The up side-down Bible

Praise for The Upside-down Bible

'This little book invites readers to take a fresh look at what Jesus actually said rather than what we imagine or wish him to have said. Its key themes of money, sex and violence are explored through stories from the gospels, all set in the context of a crash course on how to read the Bible, which is eminently readable and grounded in solid research.'

John Drane, Professor of New Testament and Practical Theology, Fuller Seminary, and Fellow of St John's College, University of Durham

'By turns provocative, passionate and kind, Symon Hill's new work is that rare thing: a book that dares to take Jesus' teaching ministry seriously. It dares to invite the reader to think for herself and be prepared to have her assumptions about Jesus, money, sex and violence turned upside-down. A must-read for anyone brave enough to explore Christianity's radical roots.'

Rachel Mann, Poet-in-Residence and Minor Canon of Manchester Cathedral

'If you're turned off by the Church but think Jesus might have been on to something – this is your book. Symon Hill reintroduces us to Jesus the teacher, whose stories don't always make easy sense because they are intended to make us instead. As always, Hill is contagiously on cue, fair and provocative.'

Mark Oakley, Chancellor of St Paul's Cathedral

'Symon turns traditional church interpretations of Jesus' teachings on their head, offering a radical reinterpretation that connects Christ's message to daily life, personal relationships and political struggles today.'

Peter Tatchell, human rights campaigner

'Jesus' stories are basically about life, not religious geekery. So what do first-timers of all faiths and none make of them? Symon Hill has listened carefully to a wide variety of people, many encountering the parables for the first time, to refresh and restore our idea of what it means to be human. He uses some knowledge from well-chosen experts, but draws us easily into the text in a playful and engaging way. The Upside-down Bible is a book of questions as much as answers, where stories we thought we knew sparkle with fresh possibilities. It invites us to dive into Jesus' teaching from many different angles, and reflect. There's something valuable here for everyone, whether complete first-timer or seasoned preacher.'

Rt Revd Dr Alan Wilson, Bishop of Buckingham

The upside-down Bible

What Jesus really said about money, sex and violence

SYMON HILL

DARTON·LONGMAN + TODD

The Upside-Down Bible is dedicated to
Shaun and Jessica, my nephew and niece,
who inspire me and give me hope for the world.

First published in 2015 by
Darton, Longman and Todd Ltd
1 Spencer Court
140 – 142 Wandsworth High Street
London SW18 4JJ

ISBN 978-0-232-53207-4

A catalogue record for this book is available from the British Library

Designed and produced by Judy Linard

Printed and bound by ScandBook AB

Contents

Acknowledgements

Much of *The Upside-down Bible* is about the reactions of people reading Jesus' teachings for the first time, as well as others coming back to these teachings and sharing their thoughts. This book would have been impossible without them. Everyone who has contributed in this way deserves a great deal of thanks.

Many of these people are quoted in the chapters that follow. Some are happy for their real names to be used, while others prefer pseudonyms or first names only. My thanks go to Adam Ramsay, Albert Beale, Alice Fleabite, Angie, Beccy Talmy, Carl Campbell, Chaminda Jayanetti, Chloe Massey, Claire Hope, Dunyazade, Elinor Zuke, Fatimah Ashrif, Frederik Kaster, Heather Burgess, Holly-Rayne Bennett, Jennifer Random, Jo Dusepo, Jon, Kyon Husseini, Pandora Blake, Paula, Sally Campbell, Samantha Tongue, Sarah Cook and Sy Parker.

I have also drawn on reactions and thoughts that have been shared in workshops, conferences, courses and online discussions. Much of this happened some time before I decided to write the book. I hope those involved will know that they are appreciated. I am grateful to the groups who organised such events and discussions, including BiCon UK, Ekklesia, the Speak network, the Student Christian Movement (SCM) and the Workers' Educational Association (WEA) as well as a number of churches and local groups.

Many thanks to my editor, David Moloney, who was always ready to answer my questions and talk things through, and to his colleagues at Darton, Longman and Todd, including Helen

Porter and Will Parkes. I am very grateful to my friend Hannah Brock for her feedback on individual chapters. She was helpful and thorough as always. The responsibility for mistakes is, of course, mine. Thanks are also due to Shaun Swann for his skill and enthusiasm in filming my vlogs to promote the book.

I doubt that I could have completed the book without the support and encouragement of friends and colleagues. Although I cannot name everyone who encouraged me, I owe particular thanks for the emotional support of Chris Wood, Lindsey Hall, Nicola Sleap and Tabitha, along with my fellow residents at Eadie Community House. Thanks to the Woodbrooke Quaker Study Centre for the excellent library, which I used often. I am also glad of several cafes and pubs in Birmingham and beyond for providing a good atmosphere in which to work on my laptop – especially the Selly Sausage and Cherry Red's.

Throughout my life, more people than I can possibly remember have contributed to my understanding of Jesus and the New Testament. I am grateful to everyone with whom I have ever talked about Jesus, whatever their views. I am indebted to the tutors and fellow students on my theology degree at Westminster College, Oxford in the late nineties, as well as on many courses since. At least as important have been my many discussions about Jesus with varied people in varied contexts: from chats with homeless Christians on the streets of London and interviews with shopkeepers in Bethlehem to the memorable experience of leading a workshop on Christianity in a fetish club and a discussion with police who were threatening me with arrest at the eviction of Occupy London Stock Exchange.

Finally, I would like to thank my parents, Ted and Madeline Hill, who brought me up to think, to question and to come to my own conclusions. As I hope this book shows, Jesus' teachings also challenge us to think. The process continues.

The Upside-down Bible

1. Reading Jesus upside-down

Jesus has been a profound embarrassment to Christianity. For the best part of two thousand years, Christian churches have produced neat statements and triumphant declarations, setting out their views of the world in finely structured formats. Often, they have forced others to accept these beliefs, bullying, bribing, beating and burning people who disagreed.

They have justified this behaviour in the name of Jesus. At times, they have discouraged people from opening the New Testament and reading the words of Jesus for themselves. Jesus' teachings are challenging, provocative and awkward. They don't fit into neat categories and well-structured theories, whether liberal or conservative, Catholic or Protestant. In the pages of the Bible, you can find a Jesus who socialised with outcasts, criticised the rich and powerful, broke the sexual conventions of his day, was rude to his own mother and was a frequent cause of confusion even to his followers. He almost never gave a direct answer to a question, often answering with another question and coming at issues sideways on.

Jesus' teachings were designed to make people think, not to shut down thinking; to encourage questions, not to provide every answer; to challenge basic assumptions and to encourage his listeners to look differently at their lives and how they related to others.

There are at least a few church leaders who would find

Christianity much easier without Jesus. He's like a socially awkward guest at a respectable dinner party, making people feel uncomfortable but too important to be asked to leave.

I write as a Christian who accepts most standard Christian doctrine. I believe in Jesus' divinity and I have faith that he rose bodily from the dead after his execution.

I don't know whether you believe these things and, on one level, I am not too bothered. That's because I want to discuss the *teachings* of Jesus.

Jesus spoke with people in the midst of their everyday lives. He talked about their concerns: food, friendship, money, marriage, love, work, morality and prejudice. He lived in a culture vastly different to our own in many ways, but in which people experienced many of the same emotions, doubts, conflicts and struggles that are part of our own lives. Today, people who might have a very polarised argument about whether Jesus is the son of God can have a much more productive discussion about the content of his teachings.

This book is based on the conviction that Jesus' teachings can still speak to people from all walks of life, regardless of whether they are religious or whether they have academic training.

Of course, we have a great deal to learn from academics, particularly those who can tell us about the historical background and the culture in which Jesus taught. But the Bible does not belong to scholars, just as it does not belong to clergy or even to Christians. It is up to you to decide how to take on board what you have read and – if you want to do so – how to apply it in your own life.

What makes this book different is that it looks at Jesus' teachings by beginning with the insights of people reading them for the first time. These can come as a shock to people who are used to hearing the passages in church and who assume that a particular interpretation is the 'obvious' or 'common sense' one.

This is a book for Christians and non-Christians, as well as those who are unsure of their views and feelings about

The Upside-down Bible

Christianity. It can be read by those who know nothing of Jesus' teachings and those who want a fresh way of looking at them.

WORSHIPPED BUT NOT FOLLOWED

Given the power of Christianity over the last seventeen hundred years, it's perhaps surprising how little attention is given to Jesus' teachings. Take the so-called 'Apostles' Creed', used by many churches as a summary of basic Christian belief. It includes these words:

> *I believe in Jesus Christ, God's only Son, our Lord, who was conceived by the Holy Spirit, born of the Virgin Mary, suffered under Pontius Pilate, was crucified, died, and was buried; he descended into hell. On the third day he rose again ...*

This creed is remarkable, not so much for what it says as for what it misses out. Christian theologian Stuart Murray says, 'I believe that Jesus was born of the Virgin Mary and I believe he suffered under Pontius Pilate, but didn't something happen in between?'[1]

Indeed it did. Jesus' teachings, not to mention most of his actions, are left out of the Christian creeds. It is in many ways much easier to talk about obtuse doctrines concerning Jesus' relationship with God than to address the thorny questions of Jesus' comments on power, poverty, wealth and women. This tendency continues. I recently came across a 'beginner's guide' to Christianity, written by a leading British theologian. It has thirteen chapters. The teachings of Jesus do not appear as a topic until Chapter Twelve.[2]

As Stuart Murray rightly puts it, for much of Christian history Jesus has been 'worshipped but not followed'.[3]

In the light of this, there are three ways in which this book approaches Jesus 'upside-down':

- Jesus' words and actions have been neglected as churches discuss Christianity in terms of abstract doctrine. The 'upside-down' approach begins where Jesus' first listeners began: with his words.

- For seventeen hundred years, Churches have been at the centre of wealth and power. Interpretations that uphold the status quo, or at least do nothing to challenge it, have become the norm. Reading 'upside-down' means recognising that Jesus mixed with poor people and outcasts and that his teachings challenged power and dominant values.

- It is often assumed that Christians who have heard the Bible read in church for years are the best placed to comment on it. I have taken an 'upside-down' approach by showing some of Jesus' teachings to non-Christians who are reading them for the first time. They have not heard sermons about them and can come to them with fresher eyes than regular readers.

I'M BIASED – AND SO ARE YOU

We all come to the Bible with preconceptions, whether or not we have read it before. There are no unbiased readers; there are those who acknowledge their biases and those who do not. The dominant views and values of any culture often seem obvious and self-evident to those who have never questioned them. Those of us who believe that Jesus sided with the poor are accused of bias, but for centuries influential writers and clerics have insisted that Jesus did not challenge political or economic systems. In effect, they are arguing that Jesus sided with the rich. But they are not acknowledging this.

This is not to say that we should just believe what we like and not worry about the evidence. Attempts to get to the truth are worthwhile, even if the truth is not what we would like it to be. While doing this, however, let's acknowledge our motives and our viewpoints – as well as recognising that we may have preconceptions of which we are not even aware.

We can all be challenged by other people's insights. In particular, those of us who are used to hearing the Bible in church can learn a lot from people approaching it for the first time. At the UK's Bisexual Convention (BiCon) in 2014, I ran a session called 'What does the Bible really say about sex?'. I was both delighted and surprised by the turnout. The room was full. Most of these people were not Christians. Some had never opened a Bible in their lives, or not since school. As bisexuals, many of them had very negative experiences of Christians who condemned them and sometimes told them they were going to hell. In that room, I felt a genuine eagerness to discover what the Bible really says.

The discussion got lively as we explored Jesus' comments on sex. In particular, we looked at what Jesus said about men who look at women with sexual desire. Some in the room found Jesus' comments liberating. Others were much more critical. Several people made observations that would never have occurred to me. (We'll be exploring the same passage in Chapter 8.)

Jesus had a great deal to say about money. Non-Christians naturally respond to Jesus' stories about money by talking about money. It may seem odd to say that Christians rarely do. They have spent years listening to sermons which suggest that when Jesus talked about money it was only a metaphor for something else. Jesus told a story about a wage dispute, but if you hear it mentioned in church, the chances are that you will be told it is a story about the grace of God. First-time readers from non-Christian backgrounds, on the other hand, respond by talking about wages. Like Jesus' original listeners, they are more concerned with the everyday necessities of life than with doctrines about the nature of God. (We will look at this passage in Chapter 4.)

On several occasions, Jesus referred to people who do not have enough to eat. If you have been in this situation yourself, it will affect how you relate to his words. If you have not, then however much you may sympathise with those who have been there, it is difficult, if not impossible, to imagine what it is like. Jesus' teachings about race and prejudice may trigger different responses from people who have been on the receiving end of racial abuse than from those who have not (more on this in Chapter 13). If I ask Christians about Jesus' positive comments about sex workers, they tend to assume that he is praising people who have *given up* sex work. I had a very different reaction when showing the same passage to sex workers (as we will see in Chapter 11).

In researching this book, I shared passages of Jesus' teachings with dozens of people who had never previously read them. On some occasions, this was in workshops and conferences. I also found volunteers on social media and sought out people with experiences and backgrounds relevant to the passages in question. They include Jews and Muslims along with members of other faiths, atheists, agnostics, some who are unsure of their religious views and a few who have recently come to Christianity.

I do not for a moment claim that these people are a representative sample of the British population. They do not represent anyone but themselves. The Jews, for example, are of course influenced by their own faith but I do not claim that all Jews would react in the same way. This is equally true for the Muslims, Pagans, atheists and so on.

When I say that these people were new to Jesus' teachings, I do not mean that they knew nothing at all about Jesus. Most people in Britain are taught something about Jesus at school, although it may be minimal and they might not remember much of it. Christian imagery and ideas are still very present in British culture.

For over a thousand years, Christianity was a dominant political, cultural and economic force in Britain. This situation is sometimes described as 'Christendom'. The word, at least in this sense, is used to describe a set-up in which Christianity is at the centre of politics and culture, and the dominant values are seen as Christian ones. Christianity's prominence in Britain, and much of Europe, has waned gradually over the last century or so. We are now in 'Post-Christendom', as Christian institutions decline in influence and as Christianity becomes less central to the country's identity.

One result of this is that far fewer people are familiar with the Bible and with what it has to say about Jesus' life. Despite this, Christian imagery lives on in British culture: almost everyone has heard the phrase 'Good Samaritan', even if they are not clear that it derives from a story told by Jesus (see Chapter 13). When I showed non-Christians a passage from the Bible about Jesus' teachings on marriage, several assumed that Jesus opposed sex outside marriage. He did not say this in the passage, although it's a possible interpretation of it. However, the readers knew that many Christians oppose sex before marriage and they assumed that Jesus would too. This is a great example of how readers' preconceptions can be shaped more by Christians than by Jesus. (We will explore this passage in Chapter 10.)

The observations of new readers are a starting point, a springboard for discussion. If you are new to Jesus' teachings yourself, you may want to consider which if any of the new readers' reactions are similar to your own. If you are familiar with Jesus, I hope these comments will provide new angles to approach the passage in question.

At this point, some will object. They will say that those with no knowledge of Jesus' historical and cultural background cannot possibly comment on his teachings. I think there is a valid point buried within this comment: Jesus' culture was very different to our own and we will understand his teachings better if we take this into account. While each chapter of this book begins with comments by first-time readers, it then goes on to explore Jesus' background and to mention what scholars have said about the passage in question.

However, Jesus' teachings continue to inspire people precisely because they relate to such common concerns as money, sex and violence. To take some of the examples that appear in this book: people alienated by religion, victims of violence, political activists, sex workers and people struggling to make ends meet probably have more in common with Jesus' original listeners than many scholars and clergy (meaning no offence to scholars and clergy!).

To put it in academic terms, we are looking at Jesus' teachings from three angles: the context of the reader, the text itself and the context in which it was written.

HOW TO USE THIS BOOK

You may be asking how we can know anything about Jesus at all. Did he really teach what the Bible says he did? Or only some of it? How do we know which parts are accurate? Did Jesus even exist?

Chapter 2 provides a brief exploration of these questions. For readers unfamiliar with Jesus or the Christian Bible, it explains a bit more about the New Testament and where Jesus' teachings can be found.

While there is no need to read this book in order, if you are unused to reading about Jesus it may be helpful to read Chapter 2 before the rest.

Most of the book is split into three themes that can be found in Jesus' teachings and that also concern many people today: Money, Sex and Violence. The themes are approximate, as many of Jesus' comments naturally cover several subjects. Each theme is divided into chapters, each based around a passage from Jesus' teachings.

This is not intended as a systematic introduction to Jesus' ideas. It is a chance to explore several of his teachings in an open-ended way. Selecting the passages has been tough, but I have tried to choose some that illustrate common themes in Jesus' teaching as well as others that are particularly relevant to controversies in our own society.

Each chapter includes these elements:

- The text of the passage (so you don't need a Bible to hand).

- Questions about your initial reactions and feelings.

- Insights from people reading the passage for the first time.

　　　　　　　　　　　　The Upside-down Bible

- A reflection on various interpretations, quoting scholars when appropriate.

- Questions about your thoughts and conclusions based on what you have read so far.

There are several ways you can use this book:

- You can read it through in order.

- You can pick out sections you are particularly interested in.

- You can read it through reflectively, perhaps taking a different section each day or each week and giving yourself time to consider the questions in detail.

- You can use it in group discussion, either working through the book or selecting the sections that seem most relevant to the group.

This book is not designed to tell you what to think. As you will realise by now, I do not claim to be unbiased. I have, for example, given more prominence to interpretations that illustrate Jesus' concern with the poor and marginalised than those that do not. This can only go a very small way towards balancing the tendency of certain others to do the opposite. But I never give only one interpretation. The book is an invitation to debate. Whatever else Jesus appealed to people to do, he encouraged them to think.

NOTES

[1] Stuart Murray, speaking on the Workshop course, London, 2008.
[2] Keith Ward, *Christianity: A Beginner's Guide* (Oneworld Publications, 2007).
[3] Stuart Murray, *The Naked Anabaptist: The Bare Essentials of a Radical Faith* (Authentic Publishing, 2010).

2. Jesus: The basics

In 2010, a theatre company advertised for a 'male white actor' to appear in a play in Trafalgar Square in London. In most job advertisements, it would be illegal to ask for someone of a specific ethnicity. Acting jobs are exempt from such laws, as producers may wish – for example – to require someone who is playing a historical figure to have the same skin colour as the person they are playing.

In this case, the 'male white actor' was needed to play the part of Jesus.

The producer Peter Hutley defended the advertisement by saying, 'Jesus was white'.[1]

I have no idea how Peter Hutley came to this conclusion. Jesus was a Palestinian Jew, who was born, lived and died in the Middle East. It is unlikely that he had pale skin.

Every culture has refashioned Jesus in its own image. In Christian art produced in China, Jesus looks Chinese. For centuries, images of Jesus in northern Europe have portrayed him as white, blond and blue-eyed. Reframing Jesus for our own culture is not necessarily wrong – if we are aware that this is what we are doing. To insist that Jesus really was white moves things to a different level. It reminds me of those nineteenth-century missionaries who failed to distinguish Christianity from western civilisation. We have made Jesus white, European, English-speaking and respectable.

This is a warning not only for traditionalists but for those of us who like to think of ourselves as more progressive. We too can create Jesus in our own image, conveniently concluding that he had all the same perspectives and personality traits that we have. If Jesus' teachings always make comfortable reading, we are probably not paying attention.

DID JESUS EXIST?

There is an ancient figure that nearly all children in Britain (and elsewhere) learn about in school. The teachings that carry his name are relayed to them, yet scholars are not even sure that they *were* his teachings. The earliest written evidence about this man was produced centuries after he lived and some question whether he even existed. Children learn about an idea named after him without the opportunity to question if he was really responsible for it.

This ancient figure is Pythagoras. The idea is Pythagoras' Theorem.

Several scholars suggest that Pythagoras was not responsible for the theorem named after him. They argue that it had already been developed and understood by others. Some of the ideas associated with Pythagoras are thought to have originated with the 'Pythagorean School' that existed after his own time. A number of historians argue that we cannot really know anything about Pythagoras at all.

I doubt that mathematicians who write about the hypotenuse of a right-angled triangle are sent angry emails from people arguing that they are wrong to attribute the theorem to Pythagoras. Those of us who write about Jesus, however, frequently receive comments from people denying his existence.

Most scholars of ancient history accept that we have more evidence about Jesus than about Pythagoras. The earliest surviving references to Pythagoras were written centuries after he is said to have lived. In the case of Jesus, the gap is about ten to twenty years.

I am *not* arguing that everything written about Jesus is true. I am simply suggesting that it would be foolish to dismiss these writings without considering them. As the historian Bart

Ehrman puts it, 'Historians can never dismiss sources simply because they are biased ... The question is not whether sources are biased but whether biased sources can be used to yield historically reliable information.'[2]

To some extent, Christians have only themselves to blame for the number of people who deny that Jesus ever lived. The existence of Jesus as a historical figure is treated as a question about faith rather than about history. The question 'Did Jesus exist?' is not regarded as comparable to 'Did Pythagoras exist?' or 'Did Robin Hood exist?' Instead it's treated as similar to 'Do you believe in God?' or 'Is there life after death?'.

This is a shame. While historians have their own biases and prejudices, they nonetheless aim to construct arguments for their conclusions that others can consider and analyse. Nearly all historians of first-century Palestine accept that Jesus existed. These include Jewish, atheist and other non-Christian historians as well as Christian ones. David Boulton is typical when he writes, 'Like Alexander the Great and unlike Adam, Jesus lived in history.'[3]

Historians disagree strongly in their views of Jesus. Some have faith in him as the son of God, others think he was a great teacher, some don't rate him highly at all. They have very different views to each other about how much of what the Bible says about Jesus is historically accurate. Yet even the most sceptical generally accept that he existed.

There has recently been a growth in online writings by 'mythicists' who argue that Jesus did not exist after all. To be fair, a few have attempted to construct reasonable arguments for this view, but it remains an extreme minority position amongst historians. Bart Ehrman wrote in 2012 that 'there is not a single mythicist who teaches New Testament or Early Christianity or even Classics at any accredited institution of higher learning in the western world'.[4] Ehrman is not a defender of Christianity. He made his name writing about bias and historical inaccuracies in the New Testament, to the outrage of conservative Christians. His vigorous defence of Jesus' existence came as an embarrassment to the extreme sceptics who had tried to use his earlier writings to insist that nothing can be known about Jesus.

The oldest surviving writings about Jesus take the form of letters, several of them written by Paul of Tarsus, an early Christian leader. Most scholars date his earliest letters to within twenty years of Jesus' lifetime. Paul talks about several of his fellow Christians as people who had known Jesus. Another early letter was written by James, Jesus' brother. If we conclude that Jesus did not exist, we must conclude either that Paul, James and the others made him up, or that somebody else wrote all these letters at a later date, cleverly leaving clues that would lead historians centuries later to date them incorrectly. Thus we are reduced to conspiracy theories.

My problem with conspiracy theories is that most people are not organised enough for a decent conspiracy. The earliest writings about Jesus reveal tensions, differences and contradictions between the various writers and within the Christian community. These differences are the very thing that undermines the argument that it was all a massive fraud. Fraudsters would not produce something so inconsistent. They would also be unlikely, when living under an oppressive regime, to invent a leader who had been executed by that very regime as a troublemaking rebel.

Some (but, to be fair, not all) of those who adamantly deny that Jesus existed are followers of 'New Atheism' and other strongly anti-religious movements. They seem to be motivated by a determination to deny any claim made by a religion. Their refusal to believe that Jesus existed is not a matter of evidence or history. Ironically, it is an act of faith.

WHAT'S IN THE NEW TESTAMENT?

Just as almost no historians argue that Jesus never lived, almost none claim that everything written about him is factually true.

Most of the surviving early writings about Jesus can be

found in the New Testament, which comprises the last part of the Bible as used by Christians. The New Testament is made up of 27 books, some of which draw on earlier writings or oral traditions. Most or all of it was written in the Middle East, southern Europe or south-west Asia. It was written in Greek, a language that was often used for international communication in that part of the world. As Jesus spoke Aramaic, some of his teachings were translated into Greek.

A fair number of people contributed to the New Testament. There are some things on which the writers agree – including the importance of Jesus. There are other issues on which they seem to have different views – such as the precise meaning of Jesus. There are also events described differently by different New Testament writers. Most of the differences are minor, but some are significant.

Does this mean these writings are useless? If we answer 'yes', we will have to argue that all writings about an historical figure are useless if they contradict each other. We would then have to throw out pretty much every biography or historical thesis ever written. If a brother and sister have different memories of the same event from their childhood, I do not immediately conclude that the event did not happen. Even those memories which turn out to be inaccurate may say something about why the event matters to them, about why they are discussing it now or about another event with which they have confused it.

There are some Christians who want you to believe that every word written in the Bible is absolutely true and that all its historical descriptions are factually, precisely accurate. This is the other side of the coin from those conspiracy theorists who believe that that early Christians were sophisticated con-artists who covered up vital facts. Both these attitudes treat the New Testament as a co-ordinated and well-structured collection of writings. It isn't.

The New Testament reveals early Christian awkwardness about some aspects of Jesus' life. Some of the writers play down elements that don't fit into their perspective or give different

The Upside-down Bible

interpretations to the same events. We can see some of these tensions if we compare different books of the New Testament with each other.

Much of the New Testament is taken up with letters written by leading early Christians to address specific problems and conflicts. The earliest were probably written in the 40s CE (Jesus was executed in the early 30s). It also includes four gospels, which are, roughly speaking, accounts of the life of Jesus. Scholars generally agree that Mark's Gospel was the earliest to be written, around forty years after Jesus' execution. He may have drawn on earlier writings. However, this was an oral culture in which oral traditions were passed down over years, probably with a higher degree of consistency than might be expected by those of us who are unused to oral cultures.

Matthew and Luke were the next gospels. They drew on both Mark's Gospel and other sources. These three gospels contain much of the same material as each other, although they often present it differently. They are known as the 'synoptic' gospels (meaning 'seeing together'). John's Gospel was probably the fourth to be written. While there is a lot of overlap between the content of the first three gospels, there is far less overlap with John. John is written in a different style and presents Jesus rather differently.

In addition to these four, there were numerous other gospels that are not included in the Bible. The majority were written some considerable time after Matthew, Mark, Luke and John and were never held in such high regard by early Christians. There are legitimate questions to be asked about how the books of the New Testament were selected. Some point to political influences on the decision. Christian writer John Henson is one of several who urges Christians to give a more important place to the *Gospel of Thomas*, one of the few gospels that may be as old, or nearly as old, as those that appear in the Bible.[5]

Henson and others are talking about 'borderline' writings: books on the fringes of the New Testament that only just made it in, or others that were left out that could have been included.

Well-known religion-basher Richard Dawkins is mistaken when he states that the four gospels that made it into the Bible were chosen 'more or less arbitrarily'. This claim was made in the nineteenth century but has since been comprehensively debunked, so it's unfortunate that the likes of Dawkins should seek to revive it. While a case can be made for Thomas and other books, most gospels were never used widely enough to stand any chance of being included. Matthew, Mark, Luke and John were treated as important by the majority of Christians long before the canon of the New Testament was finalised.

WHAT CAN WE KNOW ABOUT JESUS?

Scholars vary enormously in their views of the historical Jesus. Some believe that most of the material in the gospels is broadly true, though not every detail is true. Others are prepared to accept only the most solid facts about Jesus' life: that he was a controversial figure, was known as a healer and teacher, was involved in a conflict about the Jerusalem Temple and was crucified by the Romans.

There are several areas, however, on which most scholars agree. Some of them are particularly worth bearing in mind as we look at Jesus' teachings.

- **Jesus was a Jew.**

This is the most certain fact of all – and the one that has caused the most inconvenience. Christian rulers persecuted Jews over centuries, often backed up by church leaders. They struggled to explain away the awkward reality that Jesus was Jewish.

We have little chance of understanding Jesus if we do not recognise this. His life, faith and ethics cannot be separated from his Jewishness. His arguments with other Jewish groups were not attacks on Judaism but debates within it. He spoke Aramaic, a language more closely related to Arabic than to any European language.

Jesus' means of communication were closely related to his Jewish culture. He often responded to a question by asking another question. This style is sometimes referred to as 'Socratic', after the Greek philosopher Socrates. A number of scholars argue that it was in fact at least as common among Jews in ancient time as among Greeks.[6]

The word 'Christ' derives from a Greek form of 'Messiah'. This is a Jewish term, meaning the expected saviour and liberator of the Jewish people.

Jesus' Jewishness is relevant to every passage that we will look at.

• Jesus lived under an oppressive regime.

Jesus grew up in Nazareth, a town in Galilee in northern Palestine. He then travelled south to Jerusalem, the capital of Judea, where he was executed. Both Galilee and Judea were predominantly Jewish, but they were both part of the Roman Empire.

While Galilee had a puppet ruler, Judea was under direct Roman rule. It was run by the Roman governor, Pontius Pilate. A succession of Jewish High Priests were allowed authority over domestic affairs as long as they encouraged loyalty to the empire. Unsurprisingly, many Jews resented the Roman-backed High Priests, whom they saw as traitors and sell-outs.[7]

As we will see, Jesus' discussions often related to the power struggles of the time involving Roman authorities, Jewish leaders and Jewish rebels. We will miss out on a lot of his meanings if we do not recognise this. A few scholars, such as Richard Horsley and William Herzog, argue that Jesus deliberately made his comments slightly obtuse in order to avoid arrest. If they are right, this is one reason why he is sometimes difficult to understand!

It is worth keeping the Roman Empire in your mind whenever you are reading about Jesus' teachings. If you want to explore Jesus' attitude to Roman rule in particular, have a look at Chapters 7, 15, 16 and 17 of this book.

Jesus: The basics

- **Jesus was initially a follower of John the Baptist.**

Jesus seems to have started out as a follower of John the Baptist, who lived in the wilderness and called on people to repent of their sins, apparently inspired by the Jewish prophets of the past. John offered baptism (immersion in water) as a sign of repentance and forgiveness. Jesus was baptised by John. However, he later became the leader of his own movement. It is unclear whether this happened before or after John's arrest.

John was executed before Jesus' movement reached its height. Scholars are divided over whether Jesus saw himself as continuing John's movement or taking a step away from it. Anthony Le Donne, for example, argues that Jesus' commitment to non-violence separated him from John.[8] (John the Baptist should not be confused with one of Jesus' disciples, who was also called John – or with anyone else called John!)

To explore some of Jesus' comments on John the Baptist, see Chapter 11.

- **Jesus was known as a healer and teacher and socialised with outcasts.**

Jesus acquired a reputation for teaching and preaching his ideas, for challenging conventional wisdom in some (but not all) areas, for healing people and for exorcising people possessed by demons. He was also known for socialising with outcasts and 'sinners'.

Some of this reputation reflects the language and understandings of the culture in which Jesus lived. We don't tend to talk much about 'casting out demons' today, although mental and physical suffering remain very real. When reading about things like this, I suggest we need to avoid two temptations: taking everything literally or assuming that the understanding of our own culture is superior. Jesus' words cannot really be separated from his actions; the two went together. As we shall see, many of his teachings were spoken in the midst of action.

Jesus taught in several ways, including parables (brief stories designed to make particular points and encourage listeners to think). He said that the two most important requirements are to love God and to love our neighbours. Phrases that come up several times in his teaching include the saying 'the last will be first and the first last' (or variations on it). Central to Jesus' teachings was the announcement of a new reality termed the 'kingdom of God' or 'reign of God'. The meaning of this is contested, as we shall see.

For more on love of neighbour, see Chapter 13. On 'the last will be first,' see Chapters 4, 6 and 11. To read more about 'the kingdom of God', turn to Chapters 5 and 11.

- **Jesus was crucified by the Roman authorities.**

Jesus was sentenced to death by Pontius Pilate, the Roman governor of Judea. He seems to have been accused of claiming to be the rightful king of Judea, thus challenging the authority of the Roman Emperor. The Roman-backed Jewish authorities in Judea seem to have colluded in his arrest and execution, perhaps playing a leading part in it. However, it is difficult to determine who was responsible for what. Some of the gospels were written in the midst of Christian conflict with Judaism and some were keen to put most of the blame for Jesus' death onto Jewish leaders.

The tendency has continued. For centuries, 'the Jews' have been accused of killing Jesus. They did not. Jesus was killed by the Roman Empire. Even if a number of Jews were involved in his death, this was most likely to have been Jewish leaders who had an interest in preserving the status quo. Jesus was as Jewish as his opponents. To blame Jesus' death on 'the Jews' is as bigoted as blaming terrorism today on 'the Muslims', even when there are Muslims among the victims and most Muslims reject terrorism.

You can read more on the events leading up to Jesus' death in Chapters 16 and 17.

- **Jesus' followers believed he had risen from the dead.**

A belief in Jesus' resurrection developed quickly after his death. This was based on the experience of a number of his followers. This was a genuine belief: people don't allow themselves to be martyred for something they have made up. You might believe that Jesus' resurrection occurred as an objective event. Or you might think that those who experienced it were undergoing a purely internal psychological experience. Despite the efforts of certain people on both sides of the debate, historical evidence cannot lead us to conclusions about the truth or otherwise of Jesus' resurrection. People continue to experience Jesus today. What you make of these experiences is, of course, up to you.

- **Jesus lived at a time when politics and religion could not be separated.**

It is often said that Jesus' message was 'spiritual' rather than 'political'. There is a basic problem not only with this claim but even with this language. 'Religion' and 'politics' are our categories, the way we describe life in the twenty-first century. In Jesus' society, there was not a section of life labelled 'religious'. Religion concerned the whole of life. It was a public matter before it was a private one. Prior to the seventeenth century, there was effectively no concept of separating religion from politics.

Was Jesus' teaching religious or political? Imagine asking this question to Jesus' disciples, his opponents, the High Priest, Pontius Pilate or the passers-by who heard him

The Upside-down Bible

speaking. They would not have understood what you were talking about.

Always remember this when reading the Bible.

LEARNING FROM INCONSISTENCY: AN EXAMPLE

Let's take a look at an incident in Jesus' life that is treated differently by the different gospel writers. This might give some idea of what we can learn from Jesus even when we are not sure if we are reading a precisely accurate account.

Let's begin with Mark, the first gospel. At one point, we read about Jesus travelling to the area of Tyre – a Gentile region. He is hoping to stay there unrecognised, but fails. He is approached by a Syro-Phoenician woman who urges him to heal her daughter. At first, he refuses, making a comment about dogs that sounds like an insulting term for Gentiles. After a bit of an argument, he changes his mind and heals her daughter. According to Mark:

> He said to her, 'For saying this you may go home happy; the devil has gone out of your daughter.' So she went off home and found the child lying on the bed and the devil gone.[9]

It's a rather odd story. It is the only place in the gospels in which Jesus is shown changing his mind. The Syro-Phoenician woman is the one person ever shown to have defeated Jesus in an argument. Jesus appears to use racist language. In several ways, it's not a story that makes Jesus look very good. Mark is therefore unlikely to have made it up.

Matthew and Luke used Mark's Gospel in writing their own. They have 'copied and pasted' whole chunks of it into their own work, although often with alterations. So how do they deal with this rather awkward passage?

Matthew also includes the story, but with some added details and dialogue. There is more conversation, with Jesus offering more of an explanation for his initial refusal to help. He says, 'I was sent only to the lost sheep of the House of Israel', implying that he cannot help Gentiles as well.[10] They then have an argument along similar lines to the one in Mark's Gospel before Jesus relents. In Matthew, however, his wording is different:

> Then Jesus answered her, 'Woman, you have great faith. Let your desire be granted.' And from that moment her daughter was well again.[11]

Why did Matthew change Mark's account? He may have heard the details from someone else as well as reading them in Mark. This is quite likely in a culture full of oral storytelling. However, he may have added the extra points himself. He might have thought that giving Jesus a line about serving the House of Israel made the story clearer, or made him sound less rude. By changing the words that Jesus spoke to the woman, he put greater emphasis on faith, which fits in with Matthew's general concern to demonstrate that both Jews and Gentiles can have faith in Jesus.

If Matthew made up the extra dialogue, does this matter? If you think he was wrong to do so, would it be wrong in all cases? You could argue that it would be okay if he were changing wording to make it clearer, but not if it was done to promote his own agenda. But is the difference that straightforward? To say that Matthew was making something clearer implies that he was right in his interpretation of what Jesus was saying. Each of us can only decide for ourselves where we think the limits should lie.

What about Luke? Despite having access to Mark's Gospel, and using lots of it, Luke did not include the story at all. This may well be because it does not appear to show Jesus in a very good light. Several scholars argue that Luke was not keen on independently minded women, and this too may have influenced his decision.

The story does not appear in John's Gospel. However, it is

debatable whether the writer of John was familiar with Mark's Gospel or even knew the story. This does not apply in Luke's case.

There is an irony to all this. Luke, and many Christians today, may feel embarrassed about a story in which Jesus appears to make a racist comment and then changes his mind. But to many modern readers, it doesn't make Jesus look bad – it makes him look good. Here is someone prepared to admit that he was wrong, willing to be challenged by a Gentile woman whom he may have looked down on and to correct his behaviour accordingly. Isn't this a good thing?

By briefly examining the history of this one passage, we have looked at how gospel writers and later readers have struggled with an awkward story. We have seen some reasons why this particular story is likely to be rooted in historical fact. By asking what may have motivated the writers of the gospels, we have considered how far it is acceptable to change the details of a story. In addition, we have thought about how we and other readers might react to Jesus when reading this story today, considering both positive and negative ways of viewing his behaviour and his words.

Having used such a short passage to consider so much, I hope you will get lots out of the exploration of the passages that we turn to now. Feel free to read through them in order or to pick and choose as you wish. I have only request: please pause occasionally to consider your own reactions and to form your own conclusions. I hope you find it challenging – and enjoyable.

NOTES

[1] Tim Walker, 'Christian group's insistence on a white Jesus causes dismay', *Daily Telegraph*, 26 January 2010.

[2] Bart D. Ehrman, 'Did Jesus exist?', *Huffington Post*, 20 March 2012.

[3] David Boulton, *Who on Earth was Jesus? The modern quest for the Jesus of history* (O Books, 2008).

[4] Ehrman, 'Did Jesus exist?'.

5   John Henson, 'Firing the Canon – a personal view' in *Good As New: A Radical Retelling of the Scriptures* (O Books, 2004).

6   For example, Amy-Jill Levine, *Short Stories by Jesus: The Enigmatic Parables of a Controversial Rabbi* (HarperCollins, 2014).

7   Richard A. Horsley, 'The imperial situation of Palestinian Jewish society' in *The Bible and Liberation*, ed. by Norman K. Gottwald and Richard A. Horsley (Orbis Books, 1993).

8   Anthony Le Donne, *Historical Jesus: What Can We Know and How Can We Know It?* (William B. Eerdmans, 2011).

9   Mark 7:29–30.

10   Matthew 15:24.

11   Matthew 15:28.

The Upside-down Bible

Part One. Money

3. Trusted with money

(Luke 19:12–27)

This is a story that Jesus told. It appears, with a few variations, in the Gospels of Matthew and Luke. It is also found in the *Gospel of Thomas* and the *Gospel of the Hebrews* (which are not part of the Bible and were probably written slightly later). This is Luke's version.

A man of noble birth went to a distant country to be appointed king and then return. He summoned ten of his servants and gave them ten pounds, telling them, 'Trade with these, until I get back.'

> **Language point**
> *Pound:* This is not a pound as we understand it in Britain today. It was a large unit of currency, equivalent to about three months' wages for a labourer. In Matthew's version of the story, the currency is in 'talents' rather than pounds (this was another unit of currency at the time) so the story is often called 'the Parable of the Talents'.

But his compatriots detested him and sent a delegation to follow him with this message, 'We do not want this man to be our king.'

Now it happened that on his return, having

received his appointment as king, he sent for those servants to whom he had given the money, to find out what profit each had made by trading.

The first came in, 'Sir,' he said, 'your one pound has brought in ten.' He said to him, 'Well done, my good servant! Since you have proved yourself trustworthy in a very small thing, you shall have the government of ten cities.'

Then came the second. 'Sir,' he said, 'your one pound has made five.' To this one also he said, 'And you shall be in charge of five cities.'

Next came the other. 'Sir,' he said, 'here is your pound. I put it away safely wrapped up in a cloth, because I was afraid of you; for you are an exacting man: you gather in what you have not laid out and reap what you have not sown.'

He said to him, 'You wicked servant! Out of your own mouth I condemn you. So you knew that I was an exacting man, gathering in what I have not laid out and reaping what I have not sown? Then why did you not put my money in the bank? On my return, I could have drawn it out with interest.'

And he said to those standing by, 'Take the pound from him and give it to the man who has ten pounds.' And they said to him, 'But sir, he has ten pounds ...'

'I tell you, to everyone who has will be given more; but anyone who has not will be deprived even of what he has. As for my enemies who did not want me for their king, bring them here and execute them in my presence.'

REACTIONS

Before you continue reading, take a moment to consider your reactions to this passage. With which character do you find it easiest to identify? Why? Do the characters or the situation remind you of people or conflicts that you have encountered in your own life or in society and politics today?

INSIGHTS

Exploring this passage with non-Christian groups, I find that almost everyone gives the same answer when asked with which character they identify: the third servant.

There are strong objections to his treatment. Jennifer, reading the story for the first time, told me, 'Taking everything from someone scared and less able to think about problems is really nasty.' Dunyazade, a Muslim who recalls reading the story at school, said, 'I remember I thought it was unfair how the third servant was treated.'

Samantha, a Pagan, identifies with the third servant's fear. As a disabled person, she said it brings to mind the fear of millions of disabled people under the disability assessment regime now used in the UK. It 'passes unfair judgement, punishes them and forces them to subterfuge'.

I have never known anyone who is new to the text to say anything positive about the nobleman. One of the most amusing comments was made by an anonymous person posting on my blog site who wrote, 'I think in this parable the rich man is Alan Sugar and one apprentice refuses to take part in the challenge because it's so awful.'

A participant in a workshop I ran put it more bluntly. Asked about the nobleman, she said, 'He's a bastard.'

Jennifer was equally appalled: 'Killing people! What is with that?'

Samantha pointed to some overlooked characters: 'The bystanders protest about the ruler and his decrees, expressing shock when the last pound is given to the first servant, who now has ten cities.' She added, 'We could use them to represent the people and the media, making comment on government.'

One of Jennifer's first comments after reading the story was 'I don't get this passage at all. I don't know what Jesus is saying with it.'

Chaminda, an atheist and economics journalist, suggested that the story 'is trying to say that when powerful interests handle money, their sole pursuit is generating more money from it, and in doing so they reward those who made more money and punish those who did not'.

Jennifer wanted to know if Jesus commented further after telling the story. She added, 'I hope Jesus condemns the cruelty to the less able – and the murdering – or he's not the Jesus I've been led to believe in.'

On the other hand, Samantha believes Jesus' criticism of the nobleman is implicit in the story. She said, 'Clearly Jesus is condemning the ruler, but is he condemning the bystanders for letting things get to this point?'

Dunyazade, having not seen the passage since childhood, asked me, 'Is that really in the Bible? That the man's such a tyrant?' She remembered being told the story in a way that condoned the nobleman's behaviour.

Chaminda picked up on the statement that 'to everyone who has will be given more; but anyone who has not will be deprived even of what he has'. He said, 'That's as succinct a description of targets/bonus culture as you'll ever see!'

REFLECTION

Most Christian sermons on this parable identify the nobleman with God. This is in sharp contrast to the horrified reactions of the readers quoted here, as well as almost every other new reader to whom I have shown the text. To them, he comes across as a bully: throwing his power around, frightening the third servant and having his enemies killed.

The Upside-down Bible

Admittedly, in the version of the story that appears in Matthew's Gospel, the rich man is not quite as bad: he does not kill anyone, but he is still extremely unpleasant. Perhaps Christians are remembering their belief that God is all-powerful but forgetting the idea that God is all-loving and all-just.

Nonetheless, there are plenty of scholars who back up this approach. Some point out that in Jewish parables of the time a powerful person was a 'standing metaphor for God, who appears as a "householder" or "king"'.[1] This does not mean that it must be true in every case.

Several arguments have been advanced as to why this man *does* represent God, despite his behaviour. Some argue that what is immoral for humans is not immoral for God. This seems a hard line to maintain. Biblical scholar Kenneth Bailey argues that the third servant's description of him as 'an exacting man' was a misguided attempt at flattery, emphasising the nobleman's power and authority, rather than a description of reality.[2]

Let's remember that for centuries, interpretations of Jesus' teachings have been affected by the Church's links with wealth and power, making it more likely that a nobleman will be identified with God.

If we are seeking to follow Jesus' teaching, then how we read this story can have a big effect on our decisions about money. Nineteenth-century clergy often said that the parable showed that God will reward those who use money well. Some draw the same conclusion today. Christian investment banker Jeremy Marshall argues that 'banking is a biblical principle' on the basis of this story.[3]

A problem with this interpretation is that Jesus was Jewish. He lived at a time when devout Jews opposed usury (lending money with interest). Indeed, Christians opposed usury well into the Middle Ages. It is difficult to imagine Jesus painting usury in a positive light, even by way of illustrating something else.

Investment bankers aside, it is common these days for the parable to be used less literally. Rather than encouraging financial investment, we are told that the parable means we will be rewarded if we put our skills to good use. This is helped by the fact that Matthew's Gospel uses the currency unit 'talents' rather than pounds – which has a convenient double meaning in English.

This does not, however, explain the nobleman's violent and tyrannical behaviour. This is a problem for those preachers and commentators who believe that the nobleman represents God. One influential scholar, C. H. Dodd, described the third servant as a 'barren rascal'.[4] Like others who denigrate him, this comment flies in the face of the tendency of readers to feel sympathy for him.

So what is this story really about?

In Luke's Gospel, Jesus tells this parable shortly after encountering Zacchaeus, a wealthy and corrupt businessman. After meeting Jesus, Zacchaeus agreed to give half his wealth to the poor and pay back those he had swindled four times over. Luke presumably put these passages next to each other for a reason. I suspect it would make sense to readers such as Samantha and Chaminda, who think that Jesus is criticising the nobleman and economic inequality. Such a view has become more common among scholars, but it is still rare to hear it in church.

The parable may be a combination of two stories. Jesus' listeners are likely to have recognised the story of a nobleman going to a 'distant country to be appointed king' as a reference to Herod Archelaus. He travelled to Rome to receive the emperor's appointment to rule Judea, although his opponents sent a delegation after him, as described in Jesus' story.[5]

On this basis, we might assume that the story is a condemnation of the sins of a rich and powerful individual, but some commentators go further. New Testament scholar Richard Horsley argues that we will understand Jesus better if we look at economic developments in his society. He describes this parable as 'a miniature word-picture of the very imperial situation that had brought about a severe decline of socio-economic conditions for the Jewish people and an intensification of the divisions within the society'.[6]

The Upside-down Bible

From this perspective, the parable is a comment on the sins of inequality. This is summed up by the statement 'to everyone who has will be given more; but anyone who has not will be deprived even of what he has'.

Peter Selby, former Bishop of Worcester, differs from most church leaders in backing this interpretation of the story. He suggests that it is portraying the reality of a world serving 'Mammon' – that is, the god of wealth.[7] Elsewhere in the gospels, we can read of Jesus urging his listeners to choose between serving God and serving Mammon.[8]

Selby argues that the parable makes a judgement on the 'Mammon-driven world'. He adds, 'Knowing the world as it is makes it possible to decide to live in a different one.'[9]

How does this reading sound to you? Do you see any problems with it?

On one occasion when I blogged about this interpretation, a Christian reader commented on my blog to disagree with me, picking up on my comment that people tend to identify with the third servant. He wrote, 'Well, yes; isn't that the point? Jesus told parables mainly in order to get people to change their ways. 'He added, 'It makes sense that people who are told any parable should identify with the character who is being punished,' as this is the one who ought to change.

Is this true? If we identify with the third servant, should we consider his weaknesses and how we can avoid them?

It is possible to do this without buying into the idea that the nobleman represents God. Christian writer Andrew Parker believes that this is a story about risk-taking, about the need to do more than merely follow the rules. The third servant 'foolishly believed his job was safe' because he obeyed the rules – by looking after the money. But he did not go beyond them – by making more money. As Parker puts it, 'The man knew his boss was an out-and-out opportunistic capitalist, yet continued to think he could avoid being involved in the same game and so he buried his head (as well as the money) in the sand.'[10]

This interpretation too has its problems. Although the

third servant says he is afraid, this is not entirely borne out by his behaviour. He bluntly tells his violent master: 'You are an exacting man: you gather in what you have not laid out and reap what you have not sown.' Someone who speaks like this to a tyrant is hardly a coward! Chris Howson, a Church of England priest, suggests that Jesus is challenging us to follow the third servant's example of speaking out against injustice, rather than colluding with it like the first and second servants.[11]

This disagreement is far more than an academic exercise. How we read the parable can affect how we live, at least if we are trying to follow Jesus. It could affect our attitude towards banks, capitalism and our own money, as well as how we use our talents in the modern sense of the word. Should this parable inspire us to believe that 'banking is a biblical principle'? That we should use our talents wisely and not be fearful? That we should speak out against an economic system built on lending with interest?

It is clear that Jesus' parables were often intended as a challenge to his audience. The question is, which servant's example are we being called to follow?

QUESTIONS

1. How does our choice of interpretation affect our use of money and talents today?
2. Which servant's example should we seek to follow (if any)? How should we seek to follow it?
3. How are your answers to these questions influenced by your own economic and social status?

NOTES

[1] Gerd Theissen and Annette Merz, *The Historical Jesus: A Comprehensive Guide* (SCM Press, 1998).
[2] Kenneth E. Bailey, *Jesus through Middle Eastern Eyes: Cultural Studies in the Gospels* (SPCK, 2008).

The Upside-down Bible

3   Quoted by Jonathan Langley, 'Should we move our money?', *Christianity*, September 2012.

4   C. H. Dodd, *The Parables of the Kingdom* (Collins, 1961).

5   See, for example, Joachim Jeremias, *The Parables of Jesus* (SCM Press, 2010).

6   Richard A. Horsley, 'The imperial situation of Palestinian Jewish society' in *The Bible and Liberation*, ed.Norman K. Gottwald and Richard A. Horsley (Orbis Books, 1993).

7   Peter Selby, *An Idol Unmasked: A Faith Perspective on Money* (Darton, Longman & Todd, 2014).

8   Matthew 6:24 and Luke 16:13.

9   Selby, *An Idol Unmasked*.

10 Andrew Parker, *Painfully Clear: The Parables of Jesus* (Sheffield Academic Press, 1996).

11 Chris Howson, *A Just Church: 21st Century Liberation Theology in Action* (Continuum, 2011).

4. A wage dispute

(Matthew 20:1–15)

This is a story told by Jesus, found in Matthew's Gospel.

> **Language point**
> *Denarius:* This was a unit of currency in the Roman Empire. It was about the average daily wage for a labourer in Jesus' time.

Now the kingdom of heaven is like a landowner going out at daybreak to hire workers for his vineyard. He made an agreement with the workers for one denarius a day and sent them to his vineyard.

Going out at about the third hour he saw others standing idle in the market place and said to them, 'You go to my vineyard too and I will give you a fair wage.' So they went. At about the sixth hour and again at about the ninth hour, he went out and did the same.

Then at about the eleventh hour he went out and found more men standing around, and he said to them, 'Why have you been standing here idle all day?'

'Because no one has hired us,' they answered.

He said to them, 'You go into the vineyard too.'

In the evening, the owner of the vineyard said to his bailiff, 'Call the workers and pay them their wages, starting with the last arrivals and ending with the first.'

So those who were hired at about the eleventh hour came forward and received one denarius each. When the first came, they expected to get more but they too received one denarius each.

They took it but grumbled at the landowner, saying, 'The men who came last have done only one hour, and you have treated them the same as us, though we have done a heavy day's work in all the heat.'

He answered one of them and said, 'My friend, I am not being unjust to you; did we not agree on one denarius? Take your earnings and go. I choose to pay the lastcomer as much as I pay you. Have I no right to do what I like with my own? Why should you be envious because I am generous?'

Thus the last will be first, and the first, last.

REACTIONS

Take a moment to consider your feelings after reading this story. Which characters acted fairly or unfairly? Is your reaction influenced by your own economic situation – such as how rich or poor you are, whether you are an employer or an employee, and so on?

INSIGHTS

For some people today, the issues in the story are close to home. In many parts of the world, farm labourers and construction workers still gather in the morning to see if anyone will hire them for the day. In Britain, zero-hour contracts are very common. People await a text at six in the morning to tell them if they will have work. They are the equivalent of day labourers gathering in the market place. Jesus' society may seem very different to our own, but stories such as this one remind us of similarities as well as differences.

Nonetheless, the employer's behaviour seems odd or unrealistic to many readers. 'The passage doesn't really say why the vineyard owner keeps hiring people and paying them a full day's wage for a part-day's work,' said Chaminda, an economics journalist. 'Whether it is need for more workers, or simple charity. If the latter, it does little to reflect the reality of employer behaviour, either now or back then.'

Does the story seem relevant to people struggling with poverty and trying to get what work they can? 'I would have to identify with the late arrivals,' said Samantha. 'As a person with a disability, I have often had to claim benefits because of being unable to keep up with normal "hardworking" people.'

Jennifer identifies more with those hired in the middle of the day. 'In life in general, I think I'm hired in the third hour,' she explained. 'I'm not super good or late to the event.'

So would Jennifer be annoyed if others who did less work were paid the same amount? 'I don't think anyone was unfair in the story,' she said. 'Everyone gives what they can.' Jo found it 'difficult to say' whether anyone behaved unfairly.

Chaminda said, 'Nobody is losing out from what they agreed to work for, but those who feel they worked longest and hardest are unhappy.' He added, 'What is on one level a fair and equal settlement is instead perceived as unfair and unequal.'

Carl had a different approach. Like the others, he had not read the passage before but he reacted differently to most of them. 'The owner was unfair,' he insisted. 'Though it was generous to offer work, and though the labourers agreed to the rate of pay, they did so without full facts.'

Sally defended the workers who arrived last. 'It does not seem to be their fault that they were hired later,' she said. 'They were willing to work, but no work was available.'

The Upside-down Bible

The complaints from those who arrived first sounded familiar to many readers. Samantha said, 'This is a very emotive issue in this country right now and many take the viewpoint that the story's early starters do – that the less fortunate or able, or victims of circumstance, are inherently less deserving.'

So how does the story relate to life today? Jennifer said, 'I don't feel this story relates to current financial issues at all. It wouldn't work to pay everyone the same regardless of when they start.'

Jo suggested that 'many modern-day right wingers would refer to the story as "socialist" or "communist" in a derogatory manner'. Dunyazade said it reminded her of the communist principle of 'from each according to their ability, to each according to their need'.

Samantha said the story makes her think about social justice and the welfare state. She pointed out that everyone in the parable 'has received a decent wage to live on'. She added, 'I think the point Jesus is making is that to resent others receiving the same financial support, comfort and – ultimately – respect as you, and to consider them to deserve less of these things than you, is not a loving attitude towards others.'

It is fascinating to compare Samantha's reaction with Carl's. Both of them are on the political left and find the story to be relevant to economics today. But whereas Samantha sees Jesus advocating equality, Carl sees Jesus highlighting injustice.

'This story illustrates the exploitation of workers,' he said. 'The parallels to today are many; the inequalities of pay are vast: between genders, between different countries of the world or even areas of the same country, between workers within the same company.'

He concludes, 'Surely Jesus was saying this isn't good and that we should not behave in this way.'

Finally, it's worth noting that nearly all the comments from first-time readers related to money and work. One of the few to offer another interpretation was Sally (who does not have a

A wage dispute

religion). While most of her comments were about economics, she added, 'Perhaps it's suggesting that God will accept people into heaven no matter how long they've worshipped him.'

REFLECTION

This is a story that reads differently depending on the reader's economic situation. Most of Jesus' listeners were relatively poor. They would have been more likely to identify with the workers than the landowner.

Generations of church leaders and scholars have seen the parable differently to this. Many of them have not had to worry about finding enough work, money or food. Instead, they find doctrinal points about salvation.

Some say the parable means that those who turn to God at the last moment will be treated as equal to those who have followed God all their lives.

This is an encouraging message for many, but it is often given an anti-Semitic twist, with the first workers represented as Jews and the later ones as Gentile Christians. Methodist founder John Wesley argued that the parable's main point was 'to show that many of the Jews would be rejected, and many of the Gentiles accepted'.[1]

It is inconceivable that Jesus' first listeners could have interpreted the story in this way. While all parables have multiple meanings, there would have been little point in Jesus telling stories with no relevance to his immediate audience, most of whom were Jewish. Far from being anti-Semitic, Jesus appears to have been drawing on a Jewish tradition of 'parables of recompense',[2] in which unusual payments in relation to work were used to illustrate wider points. Jesus' story, however, goes into far more detail than most of these parables.

One recent academic commentary on Matthew's Gospel lists eight possible interpretations of this parable, none of which have anything to do with money and work. They all involve various forms of symbolism about salvation and how God

The Upside-down Bible

relates to humanity.[3] While there is nothing wrong with finding symbolism in parables, it seems a bizarre starting point. Like the first-time readers quoted above, Jesus' listeners heard a story about their everyday concerns: work, money, power, having enough to eat.

Two thousand years later, these are still central concerns for most people. How does this parable speak to us about these issues? There are at least three answers.

First, the story can be read as the Parable of the Decent Employer. From this perspective, it is advice on how employers should treat their workers. As Sally said, each worker had been willing to work all day. It was not the fault of those hired last that they had not been hired sooner. US scholar Amy-Jill Levine argues that, 'The owner is the role model for the rich; they should continue to call others to the field and righteously fulfil a contract whose conditions are from the beginning to pay "what is right" – and what is right is a living wage.'[4] She maintains that the parable 'does not promote egalitarianism' but encourages the rich to support the poor.

An objection to this idea is that it is not feasible for an employer to behave like this. As we saw above, Jennifer said it would not work while Chaminda stated that it bore little resemblance to reality. However, some say that while it is not realistic under capitalism, it would be possible under a different economic system.

This leads to the second viewpoint, which sees this as the Parable of How the Economy Should Work But Does Not. Proponents of this viewpoint welcome the story as a description of how people *should* be treated. This is close to Samantha's reaction described earlier. It can be argued that everyone should receive a living income as a right – whether or not they are able to work or to fit in with the wishes of the rich. Thomas Bohache, a minister in the Metropolitan Community Church, contrasts the system described in the parable with the society in which Jesus lived, in which 'imperial rulers and those local elites who serve them control the majority of the wealth and material possessions, while those who are the most numerous have the least'.[5]

In this case, we cannot rely on the generosity of individual employers. Errol Thompson, a Christian campaigner for economic justice, argues that we need to replace the current economic system with one based, like the parable, on 'meeting need rather than accounting for work done'.[6] As Dunyazade said, the situation described in the parable is fairly similar to an economy in which each contributes according to their ability and receives according to their need.

This approach also has its problems. The wages received by the workers seem to be dependent on the whims of the landowner. The workers are not running this system themselves. If the boss changes his mind, the workers will lose out.

A third approach is much more critical of the landowner and regards the story as the Parable of the Union-Busting Boss. This is basically the position that Carl took. Academics who share his view have suggested that the Roman occupation of Palestine led to a shortage of available territory, with many losing their land and a growing gap between wealthy landowners and poor labourers, living precariously from day to day.[7]

In the light of this, biblical scholar William Herzog insists that the landowner 'can be seen as a member of an oppressing elite class'.[8] According to Herzog, Jesus is highlighting the reality that workers' wages and chances of work are entirely dependent on the whims of the wealthy. By turning the workers against each other, the landowner discourages them from uniting in a shared interest and seeking to change their conditions.

Against this, it can be said that if a fairer system were organised, it would look pretty similar to what happened in this vineyard: people giving what they can and receiving what they need. Some might say, however, that it would feel very different if this was decided by people working together with more of a focus on need rather than money. Peter Selby suggests that Jesus was not merely criticising the landowner but the system of which he was part. As he puts it, 'The characters in the story behave entirely in accordance with what we might expect of them in a world in which the morality of money is the one that guides them.'[9]

If you hear this parable read in church, it is very likely that the sermon will say little at all about money. There are Christians who will reject all three of the viewpoints above, insisting that the story has nothing to do with money and is instead about who will be 'saved' and given eternal life.

Is this a fair distinction? It is possible to read the story recalling God's generosity and grace while remembering that God is concerned with our everyday lives and how our world functions, not merely with a distant future or an abstract doctrine.

QUESTIONS

1. Which, if any, of these interpretations do you find convincing? Why?

2. How will your interpretation affect your approach to money and work?

3. How would you discuss this story with someone in a different economic situation to yourself (e.g. much richer or much poorer)?

NOTES

[1] Cited by Amy-Jill Levine, *Short Stories by Jesus: The Enigmatic Parables of a Controversial Rabbi* (HarperCollins, 2014)

[2] Gerd Theissen and Annette Merz, *The Historical Jesus: A Comprehensive Guide* (SCM Press, 1998)

[3] W. D. Davies and Dale C. Allison, *Matthew: A Shorter Commentary* (T & T Clark International, 2004).

[4] Levine, *Short Stories by Jesus*.

[5] Thomas Bohache, 'Matthew' in *The Queer Bible Commentary*, ed. Deryn Guest, Robert E. Goss, Mona West and Thomas Bohache (SCM Press, 2006).

[6] Christianity Uncut, 'Christians urged to reject Tories and side with the poor', news release, 7 October 2012.

7 Richard A. Horsley, 'The imperial situation of Palestinian Jewish society' in *The Bible and Liberation*, ed.Norman K. Gottwald and Richard A. Horsley (Orbis Books, 1993).

8 William R. Herzog II, *Parables as Subversive Speech: Jesus as Pedagogue of the Oppressed* (Westminster John Knox Press, 1994).

9 Peter Selby, *An Idol Unmasked: A Faith Perspective on Money* (Darton, Longman & Todd, 2014).

5. Charity and justice

(Mark 12:38–13:2)

This is an account of comments by Jesus in the Jerusalem Temple. It is taken from Mark's Gospel (12:38–13:2). It appears with only slightly different wording in Luke.

Language point
Scribes: This was a technical term for certain types of Jewish religious teachers. They bore some responsibility for interpreting the law and had certain legal and political powers under the Roman occupation of Palestine.

In his teaching, Jesus said, 'Beware of the scribes, who like to walk around in long robes, to be greeted respectfully in the market squares, to take the front seats in the synagogues and the places of honour at banquets; these are the men who devour the property of widows and for show offer long prayers. The more severe will be the sentence they receive.'

He sat down opposite the treasury and watched the people putting money into the treasury, and many of the rich put in a great deal. A poor widow came and put in two small coins, the equivalent of a penny.

Then he called his disciples and said to them, 'In truth I tell you, this poor widow has put more in than all who have contributed to the treasury; for they have all put in money they could spare, but she in her poverty has put in everything she possessed, all she had to live on.'

As he was leaving the Temple, one of his disciples said to him, 'Master, look at the size of those stones! Look at the size of those buildings!'

And Jesus asked him, 'You see these great buildings? Not a single stone will be left on another; everything will be pulled down.'

REACTIONS

Which aspects of this story stand out for you? How do think that Jesus felt about the widow putting her money into the Temple treasury?

INSIGHTS

'I'm worried about the widow,' said Jennifer. 'What is the money for? It feels like a televangelist gouging the faithful.' She suggested that Jesus should have encouraged the widow to keep the money because she needed it to live on.

'She gave as much as she possibly could,' said Elinor. 'But then is it good that she did? What does she have to live on now, if she's given everything she had? And if everything she gave goes towards the upkeep of great buildings which will be destroyed, then is she going to go hungry for no good reason?'

Sally thought that Jesus was praising 'a genuine act of charity' over the gifts of rich people made for show. As a professional charity fundraiser, Sally added, 'I know that, as a proportion of their overall income, poorer people still give more to charity than rich people do'.

It can be hard to relate to something written nearly two

thousand years ago. 'Scribes' was a technical term and historians still argue over who precisely they were. Given this, it's worth noting that all our first-time readers found it easy to relate to Jesus' criticisms of the Scribes.

'Plenty of people who claim to be religious walk about in fancy clothes and sit in opulent buildings, but what do their actions and deeds show?' asked Carl. Elinor, who is a Liberal Jew, read the passage as suggesting that 'grand religious buildings are worse than pointless, because they distract from the message of the religion'.

Samantha said that exploitative leaders can be found in all religions, including her own faith, Paganism. She compared people who misuse Paganism to make money to the Scribes as described in this passage.

'Our current society treats people in poverty appallingly,' said Jess. 'Like those Scribes in the passage, our government takes from the poorest and most vulnerable people while looking after themselves and their friends.'

Samantha suggested, 'We could call this story Occupy Jerusalem. Jesus comes across as moody and rebellious.'

As Jesus left the Temple, Samantha found him 'sounding rather revolutionary, even frightening, as he tells his friends that the Temple will be destroyed'.

Others also made comments about Jesus' mood. Dunyazade thought that he appeared to be 'sarcastic'. Elinor thought he was 'masking anger'. For Jennifer, there was no 'masking' involved. She said, 'I think Jesus was very angry and agitated when he spoke. He's thinking about how things are not how they should be.'

Is there an overall message to the passage? Chaminda summed up his understanding: 'Jesus judges people on what they give up, rather than what they give.' Jess said it was about the importance of 'giving what you can and doing what you can' even when others appear on the surface to be doing more.

REFLECTION

I remember visiting London for the first time at the age of ten. I was overawed by the size of buildings: St Paul's Cathedral, Westminster Abbey, the Houses of Parliament. They were vastly bigger than anything in Daventry, the small Midlands town where I grew up. Over twenty years later, I travelled to Jerusalem and saw the Wailing Wall – all that remains of the Temple that Jesus visited. It is only one wall of the Temple yet I was taken aback by its vastness.

How impressive must the Temple have seemed to Jesus and his disciples, newly arrived from rural Galilee? Yet Jesus speaks about it almost dismissively when one of them comments on how big it is. And this comes after some controversial comments in the Temple itself.

Have you read or heard this passage before? Many people have heard only part of it, or different parts of it on different occasions. It's not often read as one narrative. The lines about the widow and the Temple treasury are often quoted in isolation.

The widow who donated her last money to the Temple is usually held up as a moral example. This is seen as a tale about how everybody's contribution matters. This can be an encouraging message, so it's no surprise that it's told in this way.

If this is the meaning, we are left with a nagging question: why would Jesus want someone in severe poverty to give her money to the Temple? Jennifer and Elinor both suggested it might have been better for the widow to keep her money. Given his teachings, Jesus would surely have thought that it was more important for someone to have enough to live on than to donate it to a religious institution.

Things become clearer when we look at the whole passage above. We see what comes before and after the story of the widow's donation. Jesus' attack on the Scribes was read by all our first-time readers as an attack on religious hypocrisy. He criticised their vanity: the Scribes want 'places of honour'. This is also an economic comment: the Scribes 'devour the property of widows'.

This is a reminder that the Scribes had political as well as religious influence. Palestine in Jesus' day was under Roman occupation. The High Priest and his colleagues were allowed a measure of domestic authority as long as they encouraged loyalty to the Roman Empire.

Scholars differ over whether the Scribes were essentially subordinate to the High Priest or whether they in practice had more freedom to disagree with the Romans.[1] The gospel writers tend to generalise about Jesus' opponents. They may have exaggerated or extended his original criticisms. Just before this passage in Mark's Gospel, we read of Jesus encountering a Scribe and praising him for his comments about the importance of love. According to Jesus, the Scribe was 'not far from the kingdom of God'.[2] So while Jesus may have opposed the Scribes generally, it seems that there were at least some individual Scribes for whom he felt some respect.

Nonetheless, Jesus is attacking people in positions of influence. This has not always been a comfortable thought for some within the Christian Church, who have instead read Jesus' criticism of the Scribes as an attack on Judaism. Some Christians have shamefully used passages such as these to criticise Jews in general. But Jesus was as Jewish as the Scribes. Many other Jews surely shared his frustration with those in authority whose actions did not match up to their words.

As several readers pointed out above, Jesus sounds pretty angry in this passage. He was 'moody and rebellious', as Samantha put it. Some scholars suggest that the words about devouring widows' houses may refer to a system whereby Scribes acted as trustees for the property of widows. It is not possible to know if Jesus had this in mind specifically.

Throughout the Bible, phrases such as 'widows and orphans' tend to be shorthand for 'vulnerable people with little or no economic support'. Some argue that the shorthand is not entirely accurate, as some widows were independent and even wealthy. Those are clearly not the sort that Jesus has in mind here. His listeners would have known God's instruction in the book of Exodus:

Charity and justice

'You will not ill-treat widows or orphans; if you ill-treat them in any way and they make an appeal to me for help, I shall certainly hear their appeal.'[3]

Biblical scholar Harry Fledderman believes that it was the cost of the Temple itself (where the Scribes 'offer long prayers') that was devouring the property of the poor, by taking money from them.[4]

Can this help us to understand what Jesus really thought about the widow putting her coins in the treasury? What if Jesus was angry about a system that pressurised the poor into giving their money to powerful institutions? This chimes with Jennifer's comment about 'televangelists gouging the faithful'.

According to New Testament scholar Addison Wright, we should see Jesus' comments about the widow not as praise but as a lament. By this interpretation, Jesus is expressing 'downright disapproval'. Wright believes that the widow 'had been taught and encouraged by religious leaders to donate as she does, and Jesus condemns the value system that motivates her action, and he condemns the people who conditioned her to do it'.[5]

Or was Jesus praising the widow's contribution as the right thing to do? Perhaps he was applauding her generosity without necessarily thinking it was wise. Can we read Jesus as cheering the widow but criticising the system? Or are the two things opposites that we must choose between?

We are not helped by the fact that most commentators either barely mention this passage or scoot over it as if its meaning were obvious. This is a legacy of centuries in which churches close to power and wealth have found it easier to read Jesus' words as comments on individuals rather than systems.

Biblical scholar Amy-Jill Levine, on the other hand, differs both from the traditional line and the idea that Jesus was denouncing the Temple system. To her, the widow is neither a passive do-gooder nor a passive victim. She argues that the widow 'retains her own income and chooses how to spend it; she has not had her house stripped from her by Scribes'.[6]

If Jesus was angry while he was in the Temple, his anger seems to have continued outside it. Some read his words about the Temple's future as a prediction of an historical event: the Temple was destroyed in 70 CE, around forty years after Jesus' time in Jerusalem. Others see an emphasis on internal spirituality rather than worship in a particular building. Several radical commentators argue that Jesus was denouncing the whole Temple system and the Jewish leadership's collusion with the Roman Empire.

Mark's Gospel was written, according to most scholars, in the late 60s or early 70s CE. This was a time of violent rebellion in Palestine. Jewish nationalists had taken up arms against the Romans and some fought to protect the Temple. According to some interpreters, Mark intended the passage to mean that Jesus would not approve, either of the rebellion itself or of the violence involved.

Let's remember that the Temple was a political as well as a religious institution. Indeed, in Jesus' time, religion and politics could not be separated (see Chapter 2 for more on this). While several first-time readers compared the Scribes to modern religious leaders, Jess equated them with self-serving politicians. If we are looking at this passage's relevance for today, how can we connect it with politics as well as religion?

One approach is to look at the motivations behind donations. To what extent are donations to charities or political parties made for purposes of securing influence or improving a company's reputation? Perhaps the rich people who put large sums into the Temple treasury are the equivalent of corporations that donate to environmental projects to 'greenwash' their image, despite pursuing policies that harm the environment.[7] How do we stop ourselves becoming so cynical that we do not recognise that some donations are made with sincerity?

The relevance of Jesus' comments seems to go far beyond

the Temple. Biblical scholar Ched Myers argues that Jesus was attacking not only the Temple system or the Roman Empire but all 'the powers of domination'.[8] Those powers are still with us.

QUESTIONS

1. Should the widow have kept her money?
2. Is it fair to compare the Scribes with religious and political leaders today? If so, which ones?
3. Jesus did not seem to value the Temple in the way that his listeners may have expected. What does this mean for how we view wealth, religion and buildings today?

NOTES

[1] Richard A. Horsley, 'The imperial situation of Palestinian Jewish society' in *The Bible and Liberation*, ed. Norman K. Gottwald and Richard A. Horsley (Orbis Books, 1993).

[2] Mark 12:28–34.

[3] Exodus 22:20–22.

[4] Cited by Ched Myers, *Binding the Strong Man: A Political Reading of Mark's Story of Jesus* (Orbis Books, 1988).

[5] Cited by Elizabeth Struthers Malbon, 'The poor widow in Mark and her poor rich readers' in *A Feminist Companion to Mark*, ed. Amy-Jill Levine with Marianne Blickenstaff (Sheffield Academic Press, 2001).

[6] Amy-Jill Levine, *Short Stories by Jesus: The Enigmatic Parables of a Controversial Rabbi* (HarperCollins, 2014).

[7] Many thanks to Hannah Brock for this suggestion.

[8] Myers, *Binding the Strong Man*.

The Upside-down Bible

6. Money and the kingdom of God

(Mark 10:17–31)

This is an account of a conversation between Jesus and a rich man. It appears in the Gospels of Matthew, Mark and Luke.

Jesus was setting out on a journey, when a man ran up, knelt before him, and put this question to him, 'Good master, what must I do to inherit eternal life?' Jesus said to him, 'Why do you call me good? No one is good but God alone. You know the commandments: "You shall not kill; You shall not commit adultery; You shall not steal; You shall not give false witness; You shall not defraud; Honour your father and mother."'

And he said to him, 'Master, I have kept all these since my earliest days.' Jesus looked steadily at him and he was filled with love for him, and he said, 'You need to do one thing more. Go and sell what you own and give the money to the poor and you will have treasure in heaven; then come, follow me.'

But his face fell at these words and he went away sad, for he was a man of great wealth.

Jesus looked round and said to his disciples, 'How hard it is for those who have riches to enter the kingdom of God!'

The disciples were astounded at these words but Jesus insisted. 'My children,' he said to them, 'How hard it is to enter the kingdom of God! It is easier for a camel to pass through the eye of a needle than for someone rich to enter the kingdom of God.'

They were more astonished than ever, saying to one another, 'In that case, who can be saved?'

Jesus gazed at them and said, 'By human resources it is impossible, but not for God: because for God everything is possible.'

Peter took this up, 'Look,' he said to him, 'we have left everything and followed you.'

Jesus said, 'In truth I tell you, there is no one who has left house, brothers, sisters, mother, father, children or land for my sake and for the sake of the gospel who will not receive a hundred times as much, houses, brothers, sisters, mothers, children and land – and persecutions too – now in this present time and, in the world to come, eternal life. Many who are first will be last, and the last first.'

REACTIONS

What is your instinctive reaction to the rich man in this story? Do you feel annoyed? Sympathetic? Indifferent? And what do you think Jesus meant by 'rich'?

INSIGHTS

Showing this passage to people unfamiliar with the Bible, I found that most had a rather negative reaction to the rich man, although some felt sorry for him. 'My instinctive attitude towards the man is that he was looking for a simple fix to make himself feel better,' said Jennifer.

Samantha suggested that the man's question ('What must I do?') implied that he thought he could make a transaction, to 'buy' eternal life in some way.

Chloe said that the rich man was 'at least *trying* to do the right thing'. On reading it again, she found him rather greedy: 'He already has wealth and power, and now he wants to live forever as well!'

Noticing the man's emotions, she added, 'I found it strange that the word "sad" was used to describe his reaction to Jesus' suggestion that he donate his own things to the poor, in that it seems such a personal and deep response. If he had been resentful, or scornful, or sceptical, there would be that level of detachment from the money itself.'

What about Jesus' attitude? Samantha said, 'Jesus seems very mysterious and a little forbidding.' Previously unfamiliar with the Bible, Samantha was finding herself surprised by Jesus' manner as she read passages for this book. 'I think I imagined him being a bit more fluffy,' she explained.

Jennifer said, 'I think Jesus foresees a place for the man in the things that were happening, if the man can make the leap to take up his place in the group.' She noted that Jesus' advice to the man is not just about giving up his wealth but about what he should do with it. She said, 'Jesus is specific about giving it to the poor. Not to the man's family or friends, or to build a temple, but to help the less well-off.'

Chloe, who has an academic knowledge of Judaism, pointed out that 'Jesus was a Jew'. She suggests that he 'expected to be argued with' because Jewish law was created through a long process of consideration, with rabbis sometimes setting out an extreme position at the beginning of a debate before compromising in the course of discussion.

So does Jesus expect all his followers to give up everything they own? Or just the rich ones?

Chloe suggested that by 'rich', Jesus meant everyone who was not 'living from hand to mouth'. Dunyazade said, 'We're rich', meaning the majority of people in Britain, when compared to most of the world.

Samantha on the other hand said, 'I feel that here Jesus is saying that persons with more than they need ought to share with those that don't. In this way nobody ever has more than they need; as soon as you did, you'd redistribute.'

Jennifer had a less literal interpretation of the word. She explained, 'By "rich", I think Jesus means attached to "stuff", unable to let go of material possessions, scared to give up the wealth and comfort they know'.

In a similar vein, Chaminda said 'the core point I take from this is the effect of wealth on the mind'. He added, 'If poverty is something to be escaped or avoided, it is not something to be voluntarily entered into, and few would choose to do so'.

Dunyazade cautiously asked, 'Can I disagree with Jesus?' She said, 'For some people it's a vocation to cast away everything but that doesn't mean it's for everybody to do.' She compared this to a commitment to celibacy, which is for those who feel called to it but not for all.

Nonetheless, she emphasised that 'I think we should all make a personal commitment to give to charity'.

Chloe suggested that the idea of giving away all possessions is 'so idealistic that people - and especially the wealthy - can safely ignore it because it seems to be so extreme'. She contrasted it to Islamic ideas about giving a percentage of your income to charity, which 'seems more achievable than impoverishing yourself'.

The Upside-down Bible

However, Chaminda said that the poor are more likely to receive help from other poor people than from the rich. He said, 'Someone who has little may be more willing to help the poor, not because he is charitable but because he sees the poor as being no different to himself'. Thus, 'It is solidarity rather than charity.'

Other readers contrasted Jesus' comments with modern economics. Carl said that Jesus' teaching seems to go against 'the type of hyper-capitalism we live under today'. After reading several passages for this book, he added, 'It also makes me laugh, and a bit irritated, that so many of those who claim to be religious are blatantly going against the Bible in their deeds.'

REFLECTION

A camel was the largest animal that Jesus' listeners were likely to have seen. They do not pass through the eyes of needles. This has not stopped rich Christians trying to force the camel through – often by coming up with ingenious twists on Jesus' words.

Sometimes it is said that the 'eye of the needle' was the name of a gate in Jerusalem, which a camel could get through but only with some effort. It's also been claimed that a 'camel' was a slang term for a thick piece of string. Looking at the meaning of words in Jesus' time is a valid activity when considering his teachings, but there is no evidence for either of these claims.

It is no surprise that some wish to soften Jesus' teaching. The Mexican theologian José Miranda writes scathingly about how the story has been twisted by 'conscience-tranquillizing' interpreters serving the interests of the rich.[1]

But what do we mean by 'rich'? Are we thinking of the very few at the top of society? Is this about the 'I per cent', to use a phrase that's become popular in global protest movements? Or should we follow Chloe's suggestion that rich is everyone not 'living from hand to mouth'? In this case, we should certainly include those on middle incomes in Britain, who are rich in global terms. More might be revealed if we look at the rich man described in this passage.

He began by trying to impress Jesus, kneeling before him and calling him 'good master'. It's no surprise that Samantha found Jesus less 'fluffy' than she expected. His response was bordering on rudeness. He may well have guessed the man was trying to flatter him and responded by not joining in the flattery.

The man is said to have 'great wealth' – or, in some translations, 'many possessions'. The original Greek words of Mark's Gospel make clear that this is not just lots of money, or a large collection of items, but property in the sense of land and buildings. The man was a landowner. Several historians believe that in first-century Palestine, Roman occupation and economic changes had led to land being concentrated in fewer and fewer hands. As the scholar Ched Myers puts it, 'landowners represented the most politically powerful social stratum'.[2]

It seems then that Jesus was talking about the very wealthy few. This has implications for how we apply the passage today.

However, many argue that Jesus' comments were more about the man's attitude than his class. The more you have, the harder it is to give up. We saw Jennifer interpreting 'rich' to mean unable to 'let go' of material possessions. Many Christian commentators have taken this line. Howard Clark Kee says that the story 'does not present an absolute denunciation of wealth; it makes, rather, a relative judgement that commitment to following Jesus must have a radical priority over devotion to one's possessions'.[3]

This principle could be extended: for some, it may be possessions that get in the way of devotion to the kingdom of God, for others it may be power, social status or some other priority that diverts them.

This may be an important point in itself, but there is a problem with the idea that this was what Jesus had in mind in this case. Once the individual man 'went away sad', Jesus talked to his disciples in terms of the 'rich'. It is only then that he used his phrase about camels and needles. It must be admitted that

The Upside-down Bible

some Christians have sought to focus on personal attachment to possessions as an alternative to questioning the economic system. Ched Myers insists that 'much more is being discussed in this story than the personal failure of this one man: judgement is being passed upon the wealthy class'.[4]

Look back at the early part of the story. Jesus says 'You know the commandments' and recites some of the Ten Commandments. But his list includes 'You shall not defraud'. This is *not* one of the Ten Commandments! It seems that Jesus (or Mark) added it in. This story also appears in the Gospels of Matthew and Luke, but in those versions the command 'You shall not defraud' does not appear. Scholars generally agree that Mark's is the earliest written version of the story, so it looks likely that Matthew and Luke both removed that line because it did not seem to fit.

So why was it included? Possibly to suggest that the man himself, by being a wealthy landowner, was effectively defrauding people. This is spelled out further in yet another version of the story. This one appears in the *Gospel of the Nazarenes*, which is not part of the Bible. It was written later than those gospels that are included in the Bible, possibly in the late second century (over a hundred years after Mark's Gospel). In this version, Jesus tells the rich man that he is not really obeying the Jewish law because:

> 'It is written in the law, "You shall love your neighbour as yourself".
> But look, many of your brothers, sons of Abraham, are clothed
> in excrement and dying of hunger while your house is filled with
> many good things, not one of which goes forth to these others.'[5]

The extra words attributed to Jesus in this version are unlikely to be historically accurate. But while they are a later addition, they indicate how the writers interpreted Jesus' response to the rich man. By this view, being rich is not compatible with loving neighbours.

With all this talk of the sins of the rich, we are in danger of forgetting something. Just as some try to water down this passage to avoid criticism of the rich, there is a risk that we

Money and the kingdom of God

could see it as a challenge *only* to the rich. If we are not part of the '1 percent', we could conclude that Jesus' words have nothing to do with us. However, the response of Jesus' disciples makes clear that they too were challenged by his comments. Their surprise may have been due to a belief that riches were a sign of God's blessing. Alternatively, they may have worried that their own decision to abandon their former lifestyle might not have been worth it.

Jesus responded by insisting that his disciples would gain far more than they had lost. This is not just in the 'world to come', when they will have 'eternal life' (precisely what the rich man had asked for). It is also for the 'present time'. Some at least have left their homes, possessions, conventional lifestyles and even their families, but now they are part of a new community that provides both food and companionship.

At several points in the gospels, it is implied that Jesus' disciples shared their property in common. This may have involved only a core group of Jesus' followers rather than all of them. It fits in with Sam's interpretation of Jesus' words to mean that people with more should share with those who have less. The theologian J. Denny Weaver, looking at Jesus' advice to the rich man, says, 'In the context of a common purse, this would not be a requirement that the man become destitute. It was rather an invitation to join the followers of Jesus, who supported each other and lived loosely to earthly wealth and possessions.'[6]

This is perhaps the hardest part of Jesus' challenge.

Throughout Christian history, there have been Christians who have sought to live in this way, sharing property in common and giving up personal possessions. They range from monks and nuns to groups who have modelled what they see as the future for the world. Not only have such groups been in a minority, but they have often attracted hostility from mainstream church leaders. The Diggers, for example, who set up common-purse communities in seventeenth-century England, were violently suppressed by the authorities of both state and church.

Our thoughts might be helped – or further confused – by

The Upside-down Bible

thinking about the 'kingdom of God' – or the 'reign of God' as it is sometimes translated. This is a central theme of Jesus' teaching in the Gospels of Mark, Matthew and Luke (although Matthew prefers the phrase 'kingdom of heaven', as his gospel was written for Jewish Christians who tended to avoid saying God's name).

This is not simply about 'going to heaven' when you die. The 'kingdom of God' refers to a new reality. Some argue that Jesus was speaking of a new society that he was trying to build or expected God to bring about in the future. Others see it as a purely internal matter, a 'kingdom of love in the heart',[7] open to anyone who chooses to live by Jesus' values.

Still others interpret the kingdom as 'now and not yet'. In this view, God's kingdom breaks in where there are acts of personal and social transformation – such as the loving of neighbours and challenges to injustice – but it is not fully realised while sin and oppression hold sway over the world.

New Testament scholar Richard Horsley writes that the passage about the rich man is only one of several in which entering the kingdom of God is identified with 'participating in the activities of a community'.[8] The community around Jesus, by sharing resources and being relatively egalitarian, posed a challenge to the dominant values of the society around it. To speak of a new kingdom naturally raises political questions in a society that already has a king – indeed, an emperor. By this reading, Jesus' call is personal, political and spiritual. As Horsley puts it, 'The old order was in fact being replaced by a new social-political order, that is, the "Kingdom of God", which Jesus was inviting people to "enter".'[9]

QUESTIONS

1. Do you feel challenged by this story? If so, how?
2. If we want to follow Jesus and his disciples, should we all pool our possessions and live in community? Or was this more useful in the time of Jesus than it is today? Or should

we focus instead on building a society in which wealth is shared? Which if any of these responses is most faithful to Jesus' teaching?

3. What do you make of the phrase 'kingdom of God' or 'reign of God'?

NOTES

[1] Cited by Ched Myers, *Binding the Strong Man: A Political Reading of Mark's Story of Jesus* (Orbis Books, 1988).

[2] Myers, *Binding the Strong Man.*

[3] Howard Clark Kee, *Community of the New Age: Studies in Mark's Gospel* (SCM Press, 1977).

[4] Myers, *Binding the Strong Man.*

[5] Bart D. I. Ehrman, *Lost Scriptures: Books that Did Not Make it into the New Testament* (Oxford University Press, 2003).

[6] J. Denny Weaver, *The Nonviolent God* (Eerdmans, 2013).

[7] Ian Breckenridge, *Reclaiming Jesus: Making Sense of the Man Without the Miracles* (O Books, 2011).

[8] Richard A. Horseley, *Jesus and the Spiral of Violence: Popular Jewish Resistance in Roman Palestine* (Harper & Row, 1987).

[9] Horseley, *Jesus and the Spiral of Violence.*

7. Taxes and oppressive rulers

(Mark 12:13–17)

This account can be found in the Gospels of Matthew, Mark and Luke. This is Mark's version (12:13–17).

Next they sent to Jesus some Pharisees and some Herodians to catch him out in what he said.

These came and said to him, 'Master, we know that you are an honest man, that you are not afraid of anyone, because human rank means nothing to you and that you teach the way of God in all honesty. Is it permissible to pay taxes to Caesar, or not? Should we pay or not?'

Recognising their hypocrisy he said to them, 'Why are you putting

Language point
Denarius: A unit of currency in the Roman Empire, roughly equivalent to a day's wages for a labourer.

Pharisees and Herodians: Political and religious factions at the time of Jesus.

Historical point
In Jesus' time, the Jews of Palestine debated whether it was right to pay taxes to the occupying forces of the Roman Emperor (Caesar). The inscription on Roman coins described the emperor as divine, which was regarded as blasphemous by Jews.

me to the test? Hand me a denarius and let me see it.'

They handed him one and he said to them, 'Whose portrait is this? Whose title?'

They said to him, 'Caesar's'.

Jesus said to them, 'Pay Caesar what belongs to Caesar – and God what belongs to God.'

And they were amazed at him.

REACTIONS

What stands out for you in this story? Why do you think that Jesus drew attention to the image and title on the coin?

INSIGHTS

Nothing is certain, said Benjamin Franklin, except death and taxes. Tax is a central political issue almost everywhere. In Britain, tax avoidance by corporations and wealthy individuals has become a headline issue, due largely to the efforts of campaigning groups.

For some, tax justice is about ensuring that all pay their fair share. For others, it is about how taxes are spent. There have always been those willing to withhold taxes in protest against expenditure to which they object, for example on warfare and armed forces.

Tax was a hot topic in Jesus' society. Taxes were levelled by an occupying power, the Roman Empire. This passage is full of subtle historical and political allusions, so it is no surprise that many first-time readers found it especially confusing. Some felt that they did not have enough knowledge to comment. Sally said, 'I'm sure there's a hidden message but I don't really get it!'

Chloe thought that Jesus was evading the question. 'He doesn't actually answer it,' she said.

Jennifer interpreted Jesus as meaning 'Pay taxes on earth, put your faith in God'.

On the other hand, Elinor, who is Jewish, said that some

listeners might believe that nothing rightfully belongs to Caesar and therefore 'interpret what Jesus said as not to pay taxes'. She added that at the same time, Jesus' comment was not explicit enough that he could be convicted of encouraging this. She acknowledged there were also several other ways of interpreting Jesus' words.

Chaminda, an atheist journalist specialising in economic issues, found that he particularly liked this passage. He thought that Jesus was talking about wider issues than whether taxes should be paid to Caesar. 'Jesus is making it plainly clear that the money demanded by the emperor is for the emperor's benefit,' he said. 'The emperor demands his money and spends it as he wishes.'

The fact that the coins described Caesar as divine, or a son of God, made Jesus' teaching more ambiguous for Carl. He found he could read it two ways: 'I think Jesus was drawing attention to the head and title on the coin to make the point that they shouldn't feel bad if they paid their taxes as the money could be perceived to be the emperor's. Equally, it could be seen that he was saying they were free to withhold it as Caesar *wasn't* the son of God.'

Some readers found links between Jesus' comments in this passage and those in the last few chapters. Samantha focused again on Jesus' manner and personality – something which had interested her since she began reading Jesus' teachings. She said that Jesus 'comes across as a mysterious renegade, canny and ambiguous – his response is like a riddle and it confuses his questioners, who he knows are trying to trick him'.

Jennifer connected this passage with the story of the rich man who wanted eternal life (see Chapter 6). Believing that Jesus wanted his listeners to pay tax, she said, 'To not pay tax is to prize the holding of money. To hold on to money is to be a "rich man" and to bar your way into the kingdom of God.'

What do Jesus' words in this passage have to say to us today?

The conclusion that Jennifer drew was, 'People should pay

their taxes regardless of their route to God, because money is earthly, for earthly things.'

Chaminda said, 'Money is a human construct, created by central government and ultimately owned by it.'

For Elinor, 'You acknowledge the rules of the country, but you can get by doing the minimum to comply with it.'

Samantha said, 'It is up to us to decide how much those who govern us are speaking for us and in our interest.' She added that we have to decide when to act if 'the emperor takes more than his due'.

REFLECTION

Jesus lived under a viciously oppressive regime. He was executed by that regime.

By the time Jesus was born, Palestine had been controlled by outside empires more or less continually for over five centuries. The Roman Empire took control in 63 BCE, around six decades before the birth of Jesus. This led to economic upheaval, violent revolt and continual political conflict. It was in the midst of this turmoil and tension that Jesus was asked for his view on one of the top political controversies of the day. He was not asked a hypothetical question about taxation, or about the relationship between religion and politics. He was asked about paying taxes to an occupying power whose ruler claimed to be divine.

We will be better able to apply Jesus' teaching to our own situation if we consider how his society was both similar and different to our own.

Jesus grew up in Galilee. By the time Jesus began his public teaching, Galilee was under the rule of Herod Antipas, a puppet ruler for the Romans. Jesus later travelled to another part of Palestine: Judea, which included the city of Jerusalem. It was in Jerusalem that he was asked this question about paying taxes, and in Jerusalem that he was later crucified by the Roman authorities. While Galilee had a puppet ruler, Judea was under direct Roman rule. It was run by the Roman governor, Pontius Pilate.

A succession of Jewish High Priests were allowed authority over domestic affairs as long as they encouraged loyalty to the empire.

Unsurprisingly, several Jewish groups resented the Roman-backed High Priests, whom they saw as traitors and sell-outs. While historians disagree over the level of support and opposition, there was a string of rebellions throughout the time of Roman rule, leading many scholars to conclude that Palestine was particularly volatile even by the standards of the Roman Empire.[1]

Not long before Jesus' time, a Jewish activist called Judas of Galilee had led a campaign by Jews refusing to pay taxes to Rome (he is not to be confused with any other Judas; it was a common name). He saw loyalty to Caesar as treachery to God. Like many other Jews, he viewed Roman coins as idols: the emperor was worshipped as a god by the Romans, and the coins carried his image, along with an inscription declaring him to be divine. To pay these taxes, said Judas of Galilee, was an act of idolatry.[2]

In such a complex situation, it is amazing that many Christian leaders today view Jesus' comments about tax as simple and straightforward. Nicky Gumbel, pioneer of the Alpha Course, insists that 'God has made it clear that we are to pay any taxes which are due. In these and many other areas, God has revealed his general will. We do not need to ask his guidance; he has already given it.'[3]

As we have seen, most first-time readers don't seem to find this passage so straightforward. For one thing, Jesus did not simply say 'yes' to the question about paying taxes. For another, his questioners must surely have expected him to say 'no', otherwise it would not have been a trap. They were 'amazed' at his answer. What was so amazing? And why did Jesus draw attention to the blasphemous description on the coin?

Jesus knew his questioners were trying to catch him out. This goes some way to explaining his behaviour. When you live under a regime that imprisons its critics, it's understandable if your comments on politics are a bit ambiguous. The slightly different version of the story that appears in Luke's Gospel says that Jesus' questioners were trying to get him arrested. He therefore seems to have gone on the offensive and challenged their own position.

Why did Jesus ask to be shown a coin instead of taking out one of his own? Some suggest that he refused to carry them, sharing the view that they were idolatrous. On the other hand, the request for a coin may simply have been a rhetorical flair. In any case, his question to his questioners exposed the fact that *they* were carrying the coins themselves and reminded them that it had a blasphemous inscription on it. As Mark's Gospel puts it, he recognised their hypocrisy.

So what did Jesus think about the original question – paying taxes to Caesar? Roughly speaking, there seem to be three possible answers.

First, some take the same view as Chloe: that Jesus was avoiding the question. This would hardly be surprising given that he was facing a trap. He pointed out the hypocrisy of his questioners – who carried the very coins they were asking about. It could be said that he turned the discussion into a challenge without stating his own position.

Secondly, many share Jennifer's interpretation: that Jesus was encouraging his listeners to pay tax. This story has often been used to encourage the idea that Christians should obey government and do as they're told. It was used in this way by Augustine of Hippo, a fourth-century theologian whose ideas did much to reconcile the Church to power, war and wealth. He said that Christians should be loyal both to the kingdom of God and the kingdom in which they live.

Interpretations such as Augustine's conveniently overlook the reality that the gospels tell of several occasions on which Jesus broke the law (see Chapter 16). Indeed, in Mark's Gospel, the story has barely begun before we find Jesus breaking the law.[4] Clergy and scholars who say that Jesus taught loyalty to the Roman regime also tend not to mention that the Roman regime executed him!

It is possible to reject the 'do-as-you're-told' interpretation while still believing that Jesus was willing to pay taxes to Caesar. We have seen Jennifer's suggestion that those who were not paying tax were prizing money. It may be that Jesus' stunt of requesting to be shown a coin was intended to point out that his listeners were happy to use the emperor's image for buying and selling. He may have been suggesting that some who withheld tax were more concerned about their own wealth than about resisting injustice.

Some scholars see Jesus as willing to pay tax not because he was colluding with injustice but because he had a different take on how to resist it. Annette Merz argues that Jesus was more concerned with contrasting the worship of God with the worship of money than with opposing Caesar.[5] The theologian Walter Wink suggested that Jesus rejected the campaign to withhold tax because it would 'change the rulers but not the rules', by replacing the Romans with a different unjust structure. Instead, said Wink, 'his assault was against the basic presuppositions and structures of oppression itself'.[6]

Thirdly, there are those who argue that Jesus *was* concerned with opposing the Roman Empire and was encouraging the withholding of tax. Elinor suggested that Jesus was implying that Caesar really deserved nothing, but avoided saying so explicitly. New Testament scholar Richard Horseley essentially takes the same view. He argues that Jesus was being ambiguous so as to avoid arrest.[7]

Jesus told his listeners to pay to God what was God's and to Caesar what was Caesar's. According to biblical scholar Ched Myers, Jesus 'is inviting them to act according to their allegiances, stated clearly as opposites'. Jesus' questioners were Jews who recognised that only God could claim their ultimate loyalty. No debt owed to God could be equated with human loyalty – let alone to a ruler who claimed divinity for himself. Myers believes that Jesus was making clear that the Roman Empire was incompatible with God's rule.

This approach encourages us to answer Jesus' question by concluding that everything belongs to God – human powers cannot demand our loyalty.

Whether or not we accept Myers' view, it serves as a reminder that Jesus' sayings were a challenge, not merely an instruction. As Samantha suggested, we are encouraged to think

Taxes and oppressive rulers

about what belongs to God, and what to Caesar – or to those who hold power in our own societies.

What conclusions can we draw for today? The story relates to lots of issues: the just and unjust use of taxes; the question of who can get away without paying tax; the need to question our real motives when we join political campaigns; the best way to resist injustice; whether loyalty to God is compatible with how we engage in politics and use money.

We have come a long way from the simple instruction that some believe Jesus' words to be.

QUESTIONS

1. Who is 'Caesar' in our own society, claiming loyalty and authority? The government? Or only oppressive regimes? Unaccountable corporations and banks, who have so much power over money? Ideas and values that are different to God's?
2. Did Jesus want his listeners to pay the tax to the emperor or not? Or was he concerned with other issues?
3. Do we have to choose between loyalty to God and loyalty to governments and nation-states?

NOTES

[1] Richard A. Horsley, 'The imperial situation of Palestinian Jewish society' in The Bible and Liberation, ed. Norman K. Gottwald and Richard A. Horsley (Orbis Books, 1993).
[2] Gerd Theissen and Annette Merz, The Historical Jesus: A Comprehensive Guide (SCM Press, 1998).
[3] Nicky Gumbel, Questions of Life: A Practical Introduction to the Christian Faith (Kingsway, 1993).
[4] Mark 2:23.
[5] Theissen and Merz, The Historical Jesus.
[6] Walter Wink, Engaging the Powers: Discernment and Resistance in a World of Domination (Augsburg Fortress, 1992).
[7] Richard Horseley, Jesus and the Spiral of Violence: Popular Jewish Resistance in Roman Palestine (Harper & Row, 1987).

The Upside-down Bible

Part Two. Sex

8. Looking at men looking at women

(Matthew 5:27–28)

T his is a quote from Jesus. It appears in Matthew's Gospel as part of a much longer speech by Jesus.

TRANSLATION ONE
You have heard how it was said, 'You shall not commit adultery.'
But I say this to you, if a man looks at a woman lustfully, he has already committed adultery with her in his heart.

TRANSLATION TWO
You have heard that it was said, 'You shall not commit adultery.' But I tell you that everyone who looks at a married woman with a view to lusting after her has committed adultery with her already in his heart.[1]

REACTIONS

What are your instinctive feelings as you read this passage? What do you think Jesus meant by 'lust' or 'a view to lusting after her'?

INSIGHTS

How is it ethical to behave when you see a stranger who you find attractive? What is it acceptable to do or not do? Does it depend on whether you are single? What if you realise the stranger is married? Is this a question solely about your behaviour, or do you need to be careful about your feelings and thoughts as well?

I often start off with these questions when I lead workshops on sexual ethics. This comment from Jesus often comes up in these sessions, as well as when I lead workshops about sexuality in the Bible.

One such workshop took place at BiCon – the Bisexual Convention for the UK – in 2014. I was delighted by how many people turned up. Very few were Christians and most were unfamiliar with the Bible. This passage divided them immediately.

On the one hand were those who found it liberating. Somebody described it as 'quite feminist'. They saw Jesus telling men not to objectify women. He seemed to be attacking sexism and sexual harassment. It seemed more progressive and encouraging than the homophobia and biphobia that some of them had experienced from religious groups.

Then there were those who found it judgemental. For them, this was about attempts to control people's emotions, to 'condemn sexual feelings' and to be negative about sex. Some saw it as similar to other judgemental attitudes that they associated with religion.

Not for the first time, we find the same passage triggering contrasting reactions within the same group of people. What is perhaps more surprising is that the split among the secular bisexual group is sometimes reflected in Christian groups.

A few months after BiCon, I led a workshop on Jesus and

sex for the Student Christian Movement. There were students present from a range of church backgrounds. Unlike the BiCon group, most of them read the Bible fairly regularly and were familiar with this passage.

One praised what he saw as Jesus' defence of 'the value of marriage'. Others said that Jesus was showing respect for women. However, one participant said that once we start getting into the ethics of 'feelings and emotions', then we can trigger 'unhealthy cycles of guilt'. Another said that this was one of the passages in the gospels that she finds 'disappointing'.

Several people in both workshops – including men and women of different sexualities – acknowledged that they found it hard not to feel sexual attraction to strangers, even when in monogamous relationships themselves. Not everyone related to this. One reader told me, 'I don't really understand having deep sexual feelings outside of a relationship.'

These varied feelings mean that some are keen to talk about translation. I have heard quite a few people say that 'lust' sounds like an instinctive feeling but that phrases in other translations imply something more deliberate. Above we read 'a view to lusting'. We could also say 'sexual desire' or 'a hope of sex'.

Within the BiCon group, some of those who viewed the passage positively said that it wasn't about judging a sexual feeling but about a decision to focus on such a feeling, which would show no respect for someone who did not reciprocate the attraction. Others were not convinced by this. In the Student Christian group, a few said that Jesus was criticising 'sexual fantasising' for someone already married, rather than involuntary emotion.

This is not the only way in which translation has an impact. The difference between 'woman' and 'married woman' is important for some. In the bisexual group, the first translation I showed them said 'married woman'. When I showed them one that said 'woman', somebody commented that she would have viewed the passage 'a lot less positively' if she had seen that one first. Several participants considered it wrong to build up a desire for someone who is committed to a monogamous relationship with someone else. But they were cautious of anything that sounded like a criticism of sexual desire generally.

In complete contrast, there are those who are *more* negative about the 'married woman' version. One atheist feminist told me that the use of the word suggests that Jesus 'thinks it's okay for men to look at *unmarried* women with the hope of sex because they are still "available" or "on the market" and not the "property" of another man'. In one workshop, a Christian feminist said that in Jesus' time, married women were regarded as the property of their husbands. 'Does this passage reinforce that idea or undermine it?' I asked. Almost in unison, someone replied 'It reinforces it', while another answered 'It undermines it'.

For some, discussions of translations and original meanings are irrelevant. 'These texts have been used for centuries to judge people,' said one Christian workshop participant. 'What matters is how we use them now.'

In a different workshop, a participant said she had been brought up in a church that used this passage to discourage any sort of physical attraction. Now, she said, she had come to realise that all people are beautiful. 'I come out of the railway station,' she said. 'Looking round, I see all these different people and I think how beautiful they all are. All of them, in their own way, are beautiful.'

REFLECTION

Christianity is in a mess about sex. Many Christian groups are torn apart by divisions over same-sex relationships. The level of sexual abuse in a number of churches has caused shock among both Christians and non-Christians. It's a surprise therefore that Jesus' teachings on sex are not often mentioned, even in discussions of what the Bible says about sexuality.

It is sometimes asserted that Jesus said nothing, or virtually nothing, about sex. It's true that Jesus seems to have said relatively little on the subject – at least when compared to his numerous comments about poverty, wealth and power. Some of his teachings are relevant to sexuality because they're relevant to all areas of life. For example, Jesus, in common with other Jewish teachers of his day, said that the two greatest commandments were to love God and to love your neighbour as yourself.[2] This teaching applies to all areas of life, so it is relevant to how we behave sexually. The Christian feminist writer Jo Ind has used it as the basis of a discussion of sex that explores how we love God, others and ourselves through our sexual behaviour.[3]

Nonetheless, Jesus did make comments that are specifically about sex and sexuality. This passage is one of them. It's a reminder of the complexity of sexual ethics. This is not simply a passage that conservatives love and liberals hate, or which feminists like but traditionalists ignore. As we saw above, it triggers opposite responses among people with similar views.

Sadly, there is one thing about which we can be sure. This passage has been used for centuries to back up views that make people feel bad about sex; not just bad about unethical or selfish sex, but negative about their bodies and sexuality altogether. This has generally had little connection with the teachings of Jesus and it has done immeasurable harm. As Pope Francis said in 2015, 'Jesus ... was far removed from philosophies which despised the body, matter and the things of the world. Such unhealthy dualisms, nonetheless, left a mark on certain Christian thinkers in the course of history and disfigured the Gospel.'[4]

Christians across the spectrum are now trying to move away from such attitudes, but old habits die hard. Some insist that they are not negative about sex but they stretch passages such as these to condemn all sorts of things that they don't mention. Christian writer Phil Moore discusses this passage with a chapter entitled 'Jesus on pornography and masturbation'.[5] He argues – or rather asserts – that Jesus' comment here means that Christians must not masturbate. This would probably have surprised Jesus' listeners (not to mention Jesus himself).

Others say that the teaching is impossible to apply because it condemns involuntary feelings. Can we resolve the question of whether Jesus was talking about an instinctive reaction or a wilful intention? In Matthew's Gospel, this passage appears as one of several comments by Jesus that all begin, 'You were told ...' and continue, 'But I say ...'. Just before his comment on adultery, Jesus is reported to have said:

> 'You have heard that it was said to those of ancient times, "You shall not murder"; and "Whoever murders shall be liable to judgement". But I say to you that if you are angry with a brother or sister, you will be liable to judgement.'

Any listener feeling smug because they have never broken the commandments was reminded by Jesus that they could break them *in their heart*. They were in no position to judge others' sin when they sometimes wanted to commit the same sin, even if they didn't put their desire into action. But what's this about being angry? Surely Jesus himself was angry? Matthew's Gospel – and all the others – present him as angry on several occasions. Jesus may have been referring to anger that was deliberately cultivated, the sort of anger you dwell on and wilfully maintain. If this is the case, then 'a view to lusting' is likewise about deliberate intention; not an instinctive feeling but a developed desire.

William Countryman is a biblical theologian whose work has made a big impact on academic understandings of sexual ethics in the Bible. He argues, both here and in other teachings, that Jesus was dismissing the notion of 'purity', by which someone became sinful or dirty solely because of a physical act. Instead, 'the purity of "the heart" is the only thing that counts'.[6]

Sexual desire is a common feature of all human societies, but Jesus' culture was very different from our own. No wonder that many want to dispense with some of the specifics of this passage and get to the general principles. Some don't want to speak in terms of gender at all. A few modern Bible translations take out all references to men and women in this passage. They speak instead of 'another's spouse'[7] or 'someone else's partner'.[8] But this misses a crucial element. There is something that it is very helpful to know about if we want to apply this passage to our lives today. Jesus was not talking only about sex. He was also talking about power.

All too often, it is women who are blamed for the sexual sins of men. In Jesus' day, women were often blamed for being a temptation. In Britain today, as in many other countries, rape victims continue to be blamed for rape: for wearing revealing clothes, for being drunk, for acting in a way that is seen by many to reduce the seriousness of the rape. Research by Amnesty International in 2005 found that over a quarter of British adults believe that a woman who wears 'sexy or revealing clothing' is partly to blame if she is raped.[9]

In this context, blaming women is an example of blaming the victim. This happens frequently in cases of sexual abuse, usually when the victim has less power than the perpetrator: because she *is* a woman, because he or she is a child, a migrant, poor or less well respected than the abuser.

In this context, Jesus told men that *they* are responsible for how they behave sexually towards women. They cannot blame the woman for tempting them, or for dressing seductively. If they develop adulterous feelings in their hearts, they have committed adultery. The Greek makes it clear that this is something they have done *to* the woman. This doesn't translate well into English, as we can't say 'he has already adulterated her'. One scholar, Kurt Niederwimmer, translates the line as 'he has already abused her by adultery'.[10]

Does this mean that only men need to take this teaching on board? As we have seen, some of those coming to this text for the first time described Jesus' comment as 'feminist', seeing it as a criticism of the objectification of women. In a society in which sexism is still rife, it can be argued that this remains the most important aspect of this teaching: a challenge to men's sexual behaviour towards women.

Alternatively, we can read it as a challenge to everyone to take responsibility for how they express themselves sexually – in thoughts, desires and assumptions as well as actions. This can only be done if we take questions of power into account, whether men's power over women, one individual's influence over another or the privileges enjoyed by certain groups but denied to others.

This approach leads to a very modern-sounding interpretation of Jesus' teaching: it's a challenge to unequal relationships, an invitation to sexual expression based on respect, consent and equality.

Some say this is making Jesus *too* modern. They argue that progressives as well as conservatives need to be careful about finding that the Bible says what they want it to. A more cautious interpretation sees Jesus as being progressive in the context of his time.

Above we read of a Christian feminist who said that married women in Jesus' day were regarded as the property of their husbands. She was right. Adultery was to some extent a property crime – the theft of another man's wife. Indeed, 'adultery' was a technical term that involved a man having sex with a married woman (a married man having sex with an unmarried woman also met with disapproval, but adultery was not the technical term for this). Some scholars, such as William Loader, argue that Jesus' comment 'does not address the rights of women' but 'has the effect of protecting male rights, the rights of the other man'.[11]

Others maintain that this does not sit well with Jesus' general disregard for property (see the Money section in Chapters 3–7). Some say that if Jesus' teaching sounds modern, it is because he was ahead of his time. In addition, Jesus' other comments on sexuality seem to pose a challenge to family structures and male headship. We shall explore this more in the next few chapters.

Where does this leave us in terms of applying Jesus' teaching today? Is it still relevant? Is it a general principle about recognising that unethical behaviour begins in our hearts? Can we draw out certain principles and if so are they about men's treatment of women, about not taking what belongs to someone else or about the need for equality in sexual relationships?

Whatever conclusion we draw, Jesus' short comment here is a

The Upside-down Bible

reminder that we cannot think about sexual ethics without thinking about power and how we – or others – use it. As the theologian Stanley Hauerwas puts it, 'Any sex ethic is a political ethic.'[12]

QUESTIONS

1. What influences your reaction to this passage? Is your response affected by your gender, marital status, sexual orientation, sexual experience (or inexperience) or by whether you have experienced sexual abuse or harassment?
2. Are you persuaded that we need to think about power relations to understand Jesus' comment? Or is this point overstated?
3. How would life be different if we sought to follow this teaching of Jesus today?

NOTES

[1] William Loader (trans.), *Sexuality and the Jesus Tradition* (William B. Eerdmans, 2005).
[2] Mark 12:28–34
[3] Jo Ind, *Memories of Bliss: God, Sex and Us* (SCM Press, 2010).
[4] Pope Francis, *Encyclical Letter: Laudato Si* (Vatican Press, 2015).
[5] Phil Moore, *Gagging Jesus: Things Jesus Said We Wish He Hadn't* (Monarch Books, 2013).
[6] William Countryman, *Dirt, Greed and Sex: Sexual Ethics in the New Testament and Their Implications for Today* (Fortress Press, 1988).
[7] Eugene H. Peterson, *The Message: The Bible in Contemporary Language* (NavPress, 2009).
[8] John Henson, *Good as New: A Radical Retelling of the Scriptures* (O Books, 2004).
[9] Amnesty International press release, 'New poll finds a third of people believe women who flirt partially responsible for being raped', 21 November 2005.
[10] Cited in Loader, *Sexuality and the Jesus Tradition*.
[11] Loader, *Sexuality and the Jesus Tradition*.
[12] Stanley Hauerwas, 'Sex in Public: How adventurous Christians are doing it' in *The Hauerwas Reader* (Duke University Press, 2001).

9. Jesus' dysfunctional family

(Mark 3:20–21, 32–35)

This is an account involving Jesus and his family. It is found in the Gospels of Mark, Matthew and Luke. This is Mark's version (3:20–21 and 32–35).

Jesus went home again and once more such a crowd collected that they could not even have a meal.

When his relations heard of this, they set out to take charge of him, they said, 'He is out of his mind.' ...

His mother and his brothers arrived and, standing outside, sent in a message asking for him.

A crowd was sitting round him at the time the message was passed to him, 'Look, your mother and your brothers are outside asking for you.'

He replied, 'Who are my mother and my brothers?' And looking at those sitting in a circle round him, he said, 'Here are my mother and my brothers. Anyone who does the will of God, that person is my brother and sister and mother.'

REACTIONS

Take a moment to consider your instinctive reactions to this passage. What's your predominant emotion after reading it? Is there anyone in the story with whom you identify?

INSIGHTS

'People who seem "mad" often have every reason to think the way that they do,' said Louise after reading Jesus' relations' belief that he was 'out of his mind'. She added that people are often described this way 'because they're the odd one out'.

For Louise, the fact that Jesus' family tried to restrain him 'muddies the issue somewhat'. Otherwise, she was generally critical of Jesus' attitude. 'He seems very dismissive of his own family,' she said, adding that he doesn't seem to appreciate 'their investment and time in him'.

Several readers felt sorry for Jesus' mother and brothers. Sally, who has recently given birth to her first child, said, 'I think I'd be pretty annoyed not to be acknowledged by my son as his mother.' Beccy suggested that Jesus' family were 'probably quite scared' by his behaviour and the likely repercussions.

Beccy, who is from a Jewish background, said that the passage shows the 'tension between being true to yourself, and your own sense of truth, and being accountable to a regulatory community, which is essentially the role of a family – to contain people'.

Louise described Jesus' words as 'well intentioned but problematic'. In his rejection of his family, he was 'almost martyring them to the cause of his ideology'.

Frederik commented, 'Many great public figures treated the

people closest to them rather badly, and Jesus is no exception here.'

What about Jesus' attitude to the crowd around him?

'What Jesus is saying feels really positive and inspiring,' said Beccy, who found his words to be 'a real relief'.

Sally was more cautious. She said, 'Viewed one way, it's very inclusive – he wants to accept people into his family.' But she added, 'If everyone becomes his brother, sister or mother, are they each individually as valued? To me, it's like performers who tell audiences "I love you all" when they've never even met people.'

Claire suggested that 'it reflects the closeness that religion provides people'. While not religious herself, she felt that 'such a community can build up a second family, and his definition of his brothers, sisters and mothers makes sense in that context'.

Frederik argued that Jesus was effectively saying, 'You are my family as long as you do what I want.' He accused Jesus of encouraging a 'personality cult'.

Beccy pointed out that Jesus had not said that his family were those who shared his beliefs but those who did 'the will of God' – which could be seen as those who acted compassionately and ethically.

Does this passage encourage people to respond positively to Jesus?

Frederik said, 'Most fundamentalist Christians overvalue and romanticise the nuclear family, if anything, so they seem to mostly ignore this passage when talking about family values.'

Claire concluded, 'It almost might suggest that religion is more important than family today, that people should listen to religion more than their own family.'

Louise said, 'I know it's supposed to read like an invite but to me it reads like an exclusion.'

Beccy commented that Jesus' comment 'feels like a really radical message and that's interesting – that it *still* feels like a radical message now'.

REFLECTION

Christianity is associated in the public mind with 'family values'. Churches in Britain that issue statements on poverty or nuclear weapons are told to 'stay out of politics', but there is an expectation that they will make comments about marriage and the family. These issues are seen almost as the churches' main remit.

So it may be a surprise to discover that Jesus was not a family man.

There are many aspects of Jesus' life on which the conclusions of biblical scholars tend to overlap with images of Jesus put forward by clergy. Issues of family are not one of them. I cannot think of any issue on which scholars differ more from popular perceptions of Jesus. It is common for mainstream biblical scholars to speak of Jesus' 'anti-family' comments. You are unlikely to hear this in church.

Conservative Christian commentators who do engage with this passage tend to pass over it quickly or try to explain it away. Guy Brandon, who makes a case for 'traditional' Christian values in modern Britain, quotes both this passage and one in which Jesus backs the commandment to 'honour your father and mother'. Taking the two together, Brandon says, 'Jesus made it clear that family was important, but that other relationships and concerns could be of even greater importance.'[1]

Is this accurate? From this passage, you might think that Jesus didn't rate his biological family at all. Louise described him as 'dismissive'. However, Brandon has a point: on other occasions, Jesus spoke approvingly of God's commandment to honour parents. Did Jesus honour his mother? He presumably thought that he did. This view was clearly not shared by some of the readers quoted above – notably Sally, speaking as a new mother.

It's not only modern Christians who find passages such as this one rather awkward. By the second century CE, Christians revered Jesus' mother Mary. His brother James, who had been one of the first leaders of the church in Jerusalem, was also highly regarded. As the historian Anthony Le Donne puts it,

'Even though they may have tried, the early Christians had very little success in suppressing embarrassing details about Jesus' life. This is especially true with his family life.'[2]

In recent years, there has been a spate of books proposing conspiracy theories about Jesus, most notably Dan Brown's *The Da Vinci Code*. It revived the old claim that Jesus was married to Mary Magdalene (who appears in the gospels as one of his followers). With no substantial evidence to back up such claims, their supporters resort to theories about large-scale cover-ups. But the survival of passages such as this one suggests that if early Christians were trying to cover up facts about Jesus' family, they didn't make a very good job of it. Ironically, some who love to promote conspiracy theories overlook the reality that the Bible already contains scandalous stories about Jesus that are embarrassing for many churches.

This passage from Mark's Gospel is not the only one in which Jesus seems distinctly unenthusiastic about his biological family. A variation of the account appears in Matthew and Luke. In John's Gospel, we see Jesus speaking rather rudely to his mother when she asks him to sort out a problem at a raucous wedding celebration.[3] He doesn't seem much more positive about her in another story in Luke

> *A woman in the crowd raised her voice and said, 'Blessed the womb that bore you and the breasts that fed you!' But he replied, 'More blessed still are those who hear the word of God and keep it!'*[4]

If you're feeling rather sorry for Mary by this point, then there is some good news. Near the end of John's Gospel, when Jesus knows he is about to die, he encourages his mother to see one of his disciples as her son, and asks the disciple to see Mary as his own mother. The disciple is said to have taken Mary into his own home. Jesus seems to have been encouraging them to look after each other as he was not able to.[5]

At that moment, then, Jesus appears to have shown more care for his family. Yet Mary was not the disciple's biological mother. Thus, Jesus was undermining biological notions of family even as he reinforced other types of family. This seems to fit in with the passage we are looking at.

Why was Jesus so negative when his mother and his brothers asked to see him? As Sally said, it is upsetting for a mother to be denied by her own son. On one level, Jesus sounds like a petulant young man who would rather be with his mates than with his parents. I hope that there is more to it than this.

Shortly before this story, Mark tells us that Jesus' family had thought him 'out of his mind' when he was preaching to a large crowd. Jesus could hardly be blamed for not wanting to see people who had just accused him of being mad. The gospels suggest that accusations of madness were made against Jesus several times, though more often by his religious and political opponents than by his relatives.

Were Jesus' mother and brothers as hostile to him as he was to them? Were they upset that he didn't want to see them? Were they motivated by a desire to protect him? Were they angry and disapproving?

Any answers to these questions are largely speculative. With Jesus being the family's eldest son, he may have been expected to take over as head of the family and fulfil domestic responsibilities, not take off for the life of a travelling activist. Was Beccy right to suggest that the purpose of families is to contain and regulate people? If so, Jesus' refusal to be contained is likely to have fuelled family conflict.

Anthony Le Donne makes the intriguing suggestion that Mary believed that Jesus was destined for high things – but that he didn't share her understanding of what that meant.[6] If your mother believes you're the messiah, this takes parental pressure to new levels! Another scholar, Ched Myers, argues that Jesus' family were frightened of the consequences of his behaviour.[7] Preaching controversial messages to crowds is a dangerous business under an oppressive regime such as the Roman Empire. The proclamation of the kingdom of God might be seen as a threat by existing rulers. The family may well have feared that

Jesus' dysfunctional family

Jesus' actions would land them all in prison, or worse.

These are only possibilities. It is hard enough to understand complex dynamics in family relationships at the best of times, let alone when trying to analyse a family who lived nearly two thousand years ago. Nonetheless, Jesus' comments in this passage give us some clues as to what he was thinking – and to what relevance this has for families and individuals today.

Jesus says that anyone who does the will of God is his 'brother and sister and mother'. The gospels give the impression that Jesus travelled around with his friends and followers while he was preaching and teaching, particularly when he journeyed from his home region of Galilee to Jerusalem (where he was eventually arrested and executed). His travelling companions seem to have included women as well as men, of different ages and possibly of varied social backgrounds. Some clearly left their families and houses to follow him (see Chapter 6). Many people are likely to have regarded this as an abandonment of responsibility. To those wedded to social norms, this behaviour would have seemed all the more shocking because of the mixture of genders, ages and social backgrounds in this relatively egalitarian grouping: they are all each other's brother and sister and mother.

They are not, however, each other's father. The word 'father' carried a rather different meaning in Jesus' culture than in our own. A family was led – indeed, it was almost owned – by its father. Wives and children were to a large extent the property of the male head of the family. Rich fathers obviously had more power than poor fathers, but even a poor father was in a socially superior position to his wife and children. The Roman Emperor was described as the 'father' of everyone in the empire.

The father is the one in charge. Jesus used the title for God alone. In Matthew's Gospel, Jesus is quoted as saying, 'Call no one on earth your father, since you have only one Father.'[8] This was a potentially subversive statement in a society built on family structures, to say nothing of depriving the emperor of one of his titles. The New Testament scholar Deirdre Good points out that Matthew in particular seems to have avoided the use of the word 'father' whenever possible.[9] Scholars of Mark's Gospel have also commented on its resistance to authority and traditional structures. This fits in with the idea of a community of equals for whom God is the only father and lord.

Not all scholars are persuaded. Tat-Siong Benny Liew writes, 'Despite all of Mark's anti-authority rhetoric ... one may question if Mark is concerned with breaking up the very make-up of authority or merely wishes to replace one authority by another.' He argues that Jesus seemed to have 'absolute authority' over his followers.[10]

Some would respond by arguing that Jesus is the son of God and that it is right he should have authority. Even if this is not something you accept, there are other responses that need to be considered. The extent of Jesus' authority over his followers may have been exaggerated in the gospels, which were written at a time when Jesus was proclaimed as the risen lord. It's also worth remembering that Jesus started out as a disciple of John the Baptist – one among many (see Chapter 2 for more on this).

Whether or not Jesus' community was as egalitarian as some would like to think, it was very likely *more* egalitarian than the society around it. It upset social values and expectations and apparently encouraged people to leave their families and conventional lifestyles in order to follow Jesus and live out the kingdom of God. No wonder Jesus' family thought he was out of his mind.

Some people still do. The well-known anti-religious writer Richard Dawkins accuses Jesus of having a 'dodgy' attitude to families. He criticises him for being rude to his mother and encouraging people to leave family behind (although he describes some of his other ethical teachings as 'admirable').[11] Despite Dawkins' supposed radicalism, it seems that his main objection to Jesus lies in Jesus' failure to uphold respectable family values.

All this raises questions about the 'family values' preaching heard in many churches. How can 'family values' be connected to Jesus' teaching? Some church leaders largely ignore Jesus' comments about his family. Others seek to downplay them. I once wrote an article for the *Guardian* in which I argued that Jesus had 'redefined family'.[12] I received an email from a reader who argued that Jesus had not redefined family, but only redefined his *own* family. Is this different? If Jesus is your brother, surely this has implications for how you see your own family as well as his.

There is an argument that Jesus was not negative about families, but only about families as they were structured in his own culture. Some say that he was hostile to hierarchy and sexism, rather than to biological families as such.

Does this argument convince you? Families in the West today are rather different to those in Palestine two thousand years ago. For one thing, nuclear families were largely unknown in that culture, in which extended family ties tended to be much stronger.

Some suggest that Jesus would be less negative about families in our society than those in his own. The implication is that families today are less hierarchical and that marriage is more equal. There is an element of truth in this claim, though there is a danger of smugness in thinking our own culture is superior. Further, while there are many happy and progressively minded families, it would be naïve and dangerous to pretend that this is universal.

In the UK today, domestic violence is still rife and most sexual abuse takes place within the family. Even in happier families, there is often pressure to conform to parental expectations. You have only to watch a few romantic comedies to see how much we are expected to live up to a romantic ideal: singleness is presented as something to be overcome, ex-partners can apparently never be friends, it is assumed that all couples want to have children and gay and bisexual people usually appear only as marginal characters.

Some common phrases in our society serve to illustrate

The Upside-down Bible

these narrow attitudes. People who are close to each other without romance or sex are described as 'just friends'. Why is friendship denigrated with the word 'just'? Were Jesus and those with whom he was speaking in this passage 'just friends'? Politicians like to say that they are supporting 'hard-working families'. Not only is this rather offensive to those who can't work (or can't find work), but it also defines people by their families. What about hard-working single people?

Was Jesus' attitude any more inclusive? We saw Frederik's suggestion that Jesus was saying his family were those who did what he wanted. Louise read his words as an 'exclusion' while Beccy found them a 'real relief'.

It perhaps depends on how we understand Jesus' statement about 'anyone who does the will of God'. Some read this as meaning those who believe in Jesus but, in this passage at least, he did not mention belief. Is it those who do as Jesus wishes? It should be noted that the gospels often portray Jesus' closest disciples as *not* doing what he wishes, but he did not abandon them. They may have been there in the circle when the message was brought in from his mother and brothers. Doing 'the will of God' could be about living ethically and lovingly rather than sharing beliefs, but is this still too narrow – or too broad? It can be argued that the boundary of doing 'God's will' was a deliberately ambiguous one.

In this passage, Jesus declares a new understanding of family at the same time as he turns away from the old one. To reject biological family is not to reject family but rather to re-make it. Perhaps Jesus was a family man after all.

QUESTIONS

1. If Jesus' family consists of everyone 'who does the will of God', who does this include? Is it about actions, beliefs or intentions?
2. Why do you think that Jesus treated his mother and his brothers as he did?

3. Should we take this passage on board when thinking about families and 'family values' today? If so, how?

NOTES

[1] Guy Brandon, *Just Sex: Is it Ever Just Sex?* (IVP, 2009).
[2] Anthony Le Donne, *Historical Jesus: What Can We Know and How Can We Know It?* (William B. Eerdmans, 2011).
[3] John 2:1–4.
[4] Luke 11:27–28.
[5] John 19:26–27
[6] Le Donne, *Historical Jesus*.
[7] Ched Myers, *Binding the Strong Man: A Political Reading of Mark's Story of Jesus* (Orbis Books, 1988).
[8] Matthew 23:9.
[9] Deirdre Good, *Jesus' Family Values* (Seabury Books, 2006).
[10] Tat-Siong Benny Liew, 'Tyranny, boundary and might: Colonial mimicry in Mark's Gospel' in *The Postcolonial Biblical Reader,* ed. R. S. Sugirtharajah (Blackwell Publishing, 2006).
[11] Richard Dawkins, *The God Delusion* (Bantam Press, 2006).
[12] Symon Hill, 'Queer, Christian and proud', *Guardian* website, 1 July 2010.

10. Redefining marriage

(Matthew 15:3–15)

This passage describes some conversations between Jesus, his disciples and his opponents. It is found in Matthew's Gospel, although parts of it are very similar to passages that can also be found in Mark and Luke.

Some Pharisees came to him, and to test him they asked, 'Is it lawful for a man to divorce his wife for any cause?' He answered, 'Have you not read that the one who made them at the beginning "made them male and female", and said, "For this reason a man shall leave his father and mother and be joined to his wife, and the two shall become one flesh"? So they are no longer two, but one flesh. Therefore what God has joined together, let no one separate.'

Language point
Pharisees: a Jewish religious and political group who emphasised strict adherence to the Jewish law.

Historical point
In Jesus' society, only a man could initiate a divorce. There was a dispute among religious teachers as to whether it was acceptable for a man to divorce his wife for any reason,.

They said to him, 'Why then did Moses command us to give a certificate of dismissal and to divorce her?'

He said to them, 'It was because you were so hard-hearted that Moses allowed you to divorce your wives, but at the beginning it was not so. And I say to you, whoever divorces his wife, except for unchastity, and marries another commits adultery.'

His disciples said to him, 'If such is the case of a man with his wife, it is better not to marry.'

But he said to them, 'Not everyone can accept this teaching, but only those to whom it is given.

'For there are eunuchs who have been so from birth, and there are eunuchs who have been made eunuchs by others, and there are eunuchs who have made themselves eunuchs for the sake of the kingdom of heaven. Let anyone accept this who can.'

Then little children were being brought to him in order that he might lay his hands on them and pray.

The disciples spoke sternly to those who brought them; but Jesus said, 'Let the little children come to me, and do not stop them; for it is to such as these that the kingdom of heaven belongs.'

And he laid his hands on them and went on his way.[1]

REACTIONS

What's your initial reaction to Jesus' words and actions in this passage? What do you make of Jesus' comments about eunuchs?

INSIGHTS

In 2012, I was invited on to Channel 5 *News* to put a Christian case in favour of same-sex marriage. My opponent, Andrew

Marsh of the right-wing lobby group Christian Concern, made a comment beginning, 'When Jesus was pressed on this issue in particular ...'.[2]

I was taken by surprise. Surely Jesus had not been asked about same-sex marriage? Andrew then went on to quote this passage. I had heard it quoted before by opponents of same-sex marriage, but never as Jesus' reply to 'this issue in particular'. As far as Andrew was concerned, the phrase 'made them male and female', said in a discussion about marriage, ruled out forever any possibility of marriage between two men or two women.

The passage has become a favourite for defenders of 'traditional' marriage, some of whom send me angry emails quoting it. They declare that the Bible has defined marriage and that we cannot 'redefine' it.

How does it sound to non-Christians who have never read it before?

'The point on divorce is possibly a historical one,' said Sarah. 'I think that marriage is best thought of as a secular agreement between two or more people who want to spend their lives together.'

Dunyazade noted that in Jesus' society, only a man could initiate a divorce. She said, 'To divorce a woman is seen as an injustice to her.' She added that she did not think divorce was always wrong, but agreed with Jesus 'discouraging' it.

Dunyazade also commented on how people 'pick and choose' from the Bible. She said that Christians who 'are not happy with people being gay' don't seem to make such a fuss about divorce, although Jesus seems to be more clearly against it.

Louise, who is not religious but is interested in exploring religion, had a very different response. She described the passage as 'harmful'. She suggested that if unchastity is the only grounds for divorce, then Jesus was saying that women's 'only worth was in their sexuality'. She worried that Christians seeking to follow this teaching would be 'a lot more likely to value chastity or fidelity over human decency'.

Another reader, Sy, noted Jesus' comment that 'not everyone

can accept this teaching'. Sy said, 'He does seem to be saying that marriage – defined as being between a man and a woman – is not expected of everyone.'

Some readers found the comment about eunuchs difficult to understand, or were unclear about the definition of 'eunuch'. Reactions varied from the very positive to the extremely negative.

'The eunuch section is really, really interesting,' said Sarah. 'It seems to say that there are people who are born agender or asexual and that is their business, and people should accept them.'

Sy, who self-defines as neither male nor female, also viewed the passage in 'a positive way' but admitted to being unsure of the meaning. 'I'm not really sure what to make of this,' said Sy. 'Whether he is referring to eunuchs as people who don't have sexual relationships, or people who aren't considered a man or a woman, or people who are not heterosexual.'

In contrast, Paula described the creation of eunuchs as 'an abusive practice'. Louise read the comment as portraying 'eunuchs as the ideal', which she considered 'very sex-negative'.

REFLECTION

Some of the passages explored in this book are rarely read other than in churches. A few are not quoted often within them. Parts of this passage, however, have been quoted many times since same-sex marriage became a hot political issue.

Let's begin with the first part: Jesus' discussion with the Pharisees about divorce. Here we see the Pharisees quoting the Law of Moses, while Jesus responds by quoting the book of Genesis. Whereas the Law of Moses is about rules for Jews, Genesis is about the beginning of the world and therefore about God's intentions for all people.

The 'traditionalist' view sees Jesus' comments as a defence of the sanctity of marriage and a championing of family values. Christian writer Guy Brandon argues that Jesus' comments 'logically imply that the biblical ideal for sex is between one man and one woman in a lifelong, exclusive relationship.'[3]

Whether we go as far as Brandon, it seems reasonable to say that the passage suggests that Jesus had a high view of marriage and fidelity and was not keen on divorce.

Down the centuries, this passage has been quoted by church leaders denying divorce even to women who were beaten, raped or otherwise abused by their husbands. The 'family values' of these people are the values of hierarchy and control, not of love and equality.

Did Jesus share this attitude? Looking at the first-time readers quoted above, Louise clearly thought that he did and objected to this passage for that very reason. Others approved of the passage because they object to casual divorce today.

We tend to speak as if 'marriage' and 'divorce' have always carried the same meaning. In reality, they have varied widely across times and cultures. Marriage in Britain today is not the same as marriage in Palestine two thousand years ago. Miranda Threlfall-Holmes, a Church of England priest, argues that we should not even use the word 'marriage' to describe them both, as they are not the same institution.[4]

Is she going too far? Whether or not we agree with her, we have to ask what Jesus' words would have meant to his listeners. Without doing so, we cannot think seriously about their usefulness today.

In that society, divorce was something that a man did to a woman. This is very far from the modern idea of a divorce by mutual agreement. Jesus was challenging easy divorce rules that allowed a man to throw out his wife on a whim. The passage might read rather differently to modern eyes if we used a different translation of the relevant word: 'Is it lawful for a man to *abandon* his wife?'

In the light of this, many readers see Jesus as an advocate of the rights of women threatened with divorce. Biblical scholar April DeConick suggests that Jesus' position 'reflected an effort to improve the quality of women's lives during his time'.[5] Another scholar, William Loader, disagrees, warning us against imposing our 'modern' ideas on Jesus.[6] It is right to be cautious, but it does seem clear that Jesus' comments would have sounded like a challenge to married men's power, at least on some level.

Some argue that Jesus was not only challenging divorce, but challenging marriage – at least marriage as it was actually practised. Elisabeth Schüssler Fiorenza, a pioneer of feminist New Testament scholarship, believes that Jesus' comment about 'male and female' was all about emphasising equality. Marriage was made for *both* of them.[7]

By this reading, Jesus mentioned gender to emphasise equality. He was not making a point about same-sex marriage – an issue that no one was raising anyway.

Male-centred divorce was only one way in which marriage was unequal and unfair. Jesus' comments are likely to have surprised his listeners for another reason. He refers to a man committing adultery after abandoning his wife. In the law of the time, the crime of 'adultery' involved a man having sex with another man's wife. His own marital status was irrelevant. The point was that he had 'stolen' someone else's wife. By suggesting that a man and woman could *both* commit adultery against each other, Jesus seems to have placed them on an equal footing. New Testament scholar William Countryman concludes that, in Jesus' teaching, 'The man ... had lost both his sexual freedom and his ultimate authority within the household.'[8]

Jesus challenged marriage and divorce as they were understood in his society. We might say that Jesus redefined marriage.

The disciples' response to his comments suggests that they, too, found them unsettling. Jesus then responded with his remark about eunuchs. Many first-time readers find this remark baffling and have no idea what to make of it. They are not the only ones.

Scholars debate the precise meaning of the word 'eunuch'. Broadly speaking, a eunuch was someone whose genitals did not conform to social expectations. They were generally seen as male but as somehow less male than other men. A eunuch may

The Upside-down Bible

have been born in this way. In some societies, he may have been castrated. Whereas most people were defined by their family roles, eunuchs were individuals. The Law of Moses made clear that men with non-conforming genitals did not have the same rights as other men in Israelite society.[9]

Theologian Megan DeFranza suggests that in Jesus' society, eunuchs were the 'quintessential other' – different to mainstream society in almost as many ways as possible. They were 'ethnically other, religiously other, sexually other and morally other'.[10]

I have heard lots of responses to the 'eunuchs' saying. Two in particular seem fairly common. Yet they are both, in different ways, fairly simplistic.

The first common response is to claim that 'eunuchs' simply means 'people who are not married'. By this reading, Jesus is saying that not everyone can accept marriage and it's okay for some to be single and celibate. This is an affirming reading for single Christians who find themselves marginalised in churches that put all the emphasis on married couples. It also fits with Jesus' challenge to dominant understandings of marriage.

However, it seems unlikely that Jesus would say 'eunuch' simply to mean 'unmarried'. Further, it does not explain the comment about people being *born* as eunuchs. In practice, this interpretation tends to be offered by those who are alarmed by the idea of Jesus saying anything positive about people who do not conform to gender norms. They are limiting his surprising saying as much as they can without denying it.

The second simplistic response is to claim that when Jesus said 'eunuch', he meant 'gay'. Keith Sharpe, a Christian writer, insists that Jesus 'is talking about perfectly normal men with a sexual orientation that is not heterosexual'.[11] I have heard others make similar claims.

This is of course an appealing message for some gay Christians. While I believe that Jesus said things that offer hope to gay people, it seems highly unlikely that he was talking simply about gay men in this passage. 'Eunuchs' were not associated primarily with same-sex relations. While the ancient world

Redefining marriage

was familiar with same-sex relations, they were not generally seen as an aspect of someone's identity. Those who engaged in them were not a separate group of people. The idea of sexual orientation did not develop until the nineteenth century.

To say that these two responses are simplistic is not to say that they are worthless. They both involve elements that are worth thinking about. It may be impossible to be certain of what Jesus meant when he talked about eunuchs, but he was clearly being positive about people who were used to being rejected because they did not conform to the norms of gender and sexuality. He may have been thinking (at least in part) about people who do not produce children. Celibate Christians *and* gay Christians can find encouragement in this, as can many others.

There are several other minorities who discuss the relevance of this passage to them. Let's take an example. Intersex people (formerly known as hermaphrodites) are born without a clearly identifiable biological sex. Their genitals may appear to be somewhere between the 'male' and the 'female', or their genitals may not 'match' other parts of their body. About one in every 2,500 people is born intersex.[12] Many are given surgery at an early age to 'correct' their genitals, although this practice is criticised by intersex rights campaigners.

Some intersex Christians identify with the born eunuchs mentioned by Jesus. Joseph Marcal says that for many intersex people 'the mere mention of eunuchs on Jesus' lips seems an endorsement of their existence and worth'.[13] The same may be true for others who don't fit into narrow gender categories. These include transgender people as well as those such as Sy, quoted above, who regard themselves as neither male nor female.

Nonetheless, it would probably be a mistake to make a straightforward equation between Jesus' 'eunuchs' and intersex or trans people, just as it is a mistake to equate being a eunuch with being celibate or being gay. But the overlaps should not be ignored.

Is it possible to be clearer about precisely what Jesus meant? Scholars have made some suggestions. William Countryman believes that Jesus' earlier comments – prohibiting divorce and implying sexual equality in marriage – were calling on men to give up their traditional role and therefore effectively becoming 'eunuchs' for the kingdom of heaven.[14]

Halvor Moxnes suggests that 'eunuch' was used as an insult against the young men in Jesus' movement who had left homes and families to follow him, giving up traditional roles and posing 'a provocation to the very order of the community'.[15] According to this theory, Jesus was 'reclaiming' the word 'eunuch' in much the same way that some people have reclaimed the word 'queer'.

Do you find either of these theories convincing? They both involve a fair bit of speculation. We may have to conclude that it is not possible to be sure of Jesus' meaning. The one thing we can say is that Jesus is speaking positively about people who were marginalised because they did not fit into expectations about gender, sexuality and family.

The passage concludes with Jesus treating children with respect and insisting that the kingdom of heaven belongs to 'such as these'. Children were the least important people. They were the property of their fathers. The kingdom of God, it seems, belongs to those deemed least important. The family becomes another social institution turned upside-down by Jesus.

QUESTIONS

1. Was Jesus upholding family values? If so, what sort of family values?
2. What would Jesus say about marriage and divorce in today's society?
3. What relevance, if any, does this passage have for debates about same-sex marriage?

NOTES

[1] This translation is from the New Revised Standard Version (Anglicized).

[2] Channel 5 *News*, 12 June 2012. The discussion can be viewed on Christian Concern's website: http://www.christianconcern.com/media/channel-five-news-andrew-marsh-of-christian-concern-and-symon-hill-from-ekklesia-on-same-sex-m (accessed 2 August 2015).

[3] Guy Brandon, *Just Sex: Is it Ever Just Sex?* (IVP, 2009).

[4] Miranda Threlfall-Holmes, speaking at the Greenbelt festival, 22 August 2014.

[5] April D. DeConick, *Holy Misogyny: Why the Sex and Gender Conflicts in the Early Church Still Matter* (Bloomsbury, 2013).

[6] William Loader, *Sexuality and the Jesus Tradition* (William B. Eerdmans, 2005).

[7] Elisabeth Schüssler Fiorenza, *In Memory of Her: A Feminist Theological Reconstruction of Christian Origins* (SCM Press, 1983).

[8] William Countryman, *Dirt, Greed and Sex: Sexual Ethics in the New Testament and their Implications for Today* (Fortress Press, 1988).

[9] Deuteronomy 23:2.

[10] Megan K. DeFranza, 'Troubling conservative and queer readings of intersex and the Bible' in *Intersex, Theology and the Bible: Troubling Bodies in Church, Text and Society*, ed. Susannah Cornwall (Palgrave Macmillan, 2015).

[11] Keith Sharpe, *The Gay Gospels: Good News for Lesbian, Gay, Bisexual and Transgendered People* (O Books, 2011).

[12] Susannah Cornwall, *Sex and Uncertainty in the Body of Christ: Intersex Conditions and Christian Theology* (Routledge, 2010).

[13] Joseph A. Marcal, 'Who are you calling a eunuch?! Staging conversations and connections between feminist and queer biblical studies and intersex advocacy' in *Intersex, Theology and the Bible, ed.* Cornwall.

[14] Countryman, *Dirt, Greed and Sex*.

[15] Halvor Moxnes, *Putting Jesus in His Place: A Radical Vision of Household and Kingdom* (Westminster John Knox Press, 2003).

11. Sex workers in the kingdom of God

(Matthew 21:22–32)

This is an account of an argument involving Jesus, as it appears in Matthew's Gospel (21:22–32).

He had gone into the Temple and was teaching, when the chief priests and the elders of the people came to him and said, 'What authority have you for acting like this? And who gave you this authority?'

In reply Jesus said to them, 'And I will ask you a question, just one; if you tell me the answer to it, then I will tell you my authority for acting like this. John's baptism, what was its origin, heavenly or human?'

Language point

Pharisees: A Jewish religious and political group who emphasised strict adherence to the Jewish law.

John the Baptist: A religious teacher of whom Jesus had previously been a follower. He denounced corruption and oppression and had since been executed.

Historical point

The Roman authorities who were occupying Palestine at this time hired local business people as agents to collect taxes. These agents then employed local tax-collectors.

And they argued this way among themselves, 'If we say heavenly, he will retort to us, "Then why did you refuse to believe him?"; but if we say human, we have the people to fear, for they all hold that John was a prophet.'

So their reply to Jesus was, 'We do not know.'

And he retorted to them, 'Nor will I tell you my authority for acting like this.'

'What is your opinion? A man had two sons. He went and said to the first, "My boy, go and work in the vineyard today." He answered, "I will not go," but afterwards thought better of it and went. The man then went and said the same thing to the second who answered, "Certainly, sir," but did not go. Which of the two did the father's will?'

They said, 'The first.'

Jesus said to them, 'In truth I tell you, tax collectors and prostitutes are making their way into the kingdom of God before you. For John came to you, showing the way of righteousness, but you did not believe him, and yet the tax collectors and prostitutes did. Even after seeing that, you refused to think better of it and believe in him.'

REACTIONS
What are your emotions after reading this passage. How do you feel about the 'tax collectors and prostitutes'?

INSIGHTS
'A sex worker who has faith is more godly than a priest who doesn't,' said Pandora after reading this passage. She's a sex

worker, and had a positive response to Jesus' words here.

'No one can know for sure whether John or Jesus had authority from heaven,' she said. 'It's a matter of faith'. She distinguished faith from 'blindly following tradition', adding, 'It's better to be open-minded to see the divine where you can, than be dogmatic and claim to be religious while rejecting the works of God because they don't fit your preconceptions. Sex workers are a good metaphor for this because we are a marginalised class of people in most societies.'

Sarah, who has been a sex worker in the past, was not quite as enthusiastic. She said, 'I get that it is saying redemption is possible for all people no matter how socially disliked.' But she asked, 'Is it saying that sex work is a "sin" and can only be made better by turning to that God?'

Several other readers found Jesus unclear. Sally described his response as 'evasive'. Claire said he was 'obtuse'.

Sally found that Jesus 'comes across as a bit superior'. In contrast, Pandora felt that Jesus had 'immediately asserted his authority'. Beccy said, 'This is another story where they're trying to trap Jesus and he's trying to find a way out.'

Beccy, a Quaker from a Jewish background, was getting used to reading the New Testament. Along with some other passages, this one affected her perceptions of Jesus. She had not previously thought of Jesus as 'a clever orator' but as someone 'speaking from the heart'. She now noticed a tension between Jesus 'saying quite shocking and outlandish things and getting himself into trouble and being quite clever about it and able to get himself out of a tight corner'.

Why mention tax collectors and sex workers? 'Because those were people who were not thought well of in that society,' suggested Sy. Pandora said, 'Jesus is saying that social acceptability is not a factor in godliness, or goodness.' Beccy thought the phrase was meant to refer to people low down in the social order who 'have the potential to be faithful and loving and on the right course' just as much as those who are more respected or better off.

Sy added that Jesus was not concerned with outward appearance or whatever happens to be fashionable but with 'how you think and feel and follow his teachings'.

However, Claire found herself disagreeing with Jesus, particularly his parable about the man with two sons. She said the parable was about distinguishing between actions and intentions and 'it seems as if Jesus believes intent is irrelevant'. In contrast, Claire believes that intentions are 'an important part of interactions between people'.

While generally very positive about the passage, Pandora felt uncomfortable with sex workers being grouped with tax collectors. Initially, she said, 'Tax collectors are class traitors who grow their wealth at the expense of the oppressed.' However, she then acknowledged that tax collectors might themselves be poor and taking the work out of desperation. She said that sex workers' clients are usually wealthy. Therefore, 'sex workers tap the resources of those in power to survive; tax collectors tap the resources of the powerless to survive, in a way that actively contributes to their oppression'.

Sarah concluded with a crucial question: 'Do the sex workers still get to be sex workers *and* followers of that God?' She added, 'I would like to think so.'

REFLECTION

Most commentators don't have a great deal to say about sex workers and tax collectors. They tend to focus on Jesus' interaction with the Pharisees.

As Beccy pointed out, this was one of many occasions on which Jesus turned the tables on his adversaries with a clever response to a challenge. They wanted him to say with what authority he was acting. It's a fair question. According to Matthew's Gospel, this conversation came shortly after Jesus had led a major protest in the Temple (more on this in Chapter 16). He then encouraged poor people into the Temple, along with disabled people and children, who were not generally allowed there. What's his authority for all this?

It seems that Jesus did not want to say that he was acting with God's authority. Was he not sure that he was? Or was he avoiding an arrest for blasphemy? Perhaps he wanted people to judge his teachings and his actions on their own terms? It may be that his own question is a subtle answer to the Pharisees' question: he was implying that he had the same authority as John the Baptist.

This time, Jesus produces a comical situation. After the Pharisees refuse to say where John's authority came from, Jesus basically says 'Well, I'm not going to tell you either!' He then pushes on with a quick-fire parable about a man with two sons. He asks the Pharisees whether the son who did the father's will was the one who acted on his request or the one who only said that he would. The Pharisees have little choice but to give the obvious answer.

Like a number of other parables (see Chapter 4 and Chapter 13), this one has been twisted by generations of Christians to make anti-Jewish points. John Chrysostom, Archbishop of Constantinople in the fourth century, believed that the parable shows 'what came to pass with respect to both the Gentiles and the Jews'.[1] To Chrysostom, the first son represents Gentiles who obey God while the second son stands for Jews, who claim to follow God's law but do not.

This influential interpretation overlooks the words of Jesus after the parable. He does not compare the Pharisees with Gentiles, but with tax collectors and sex workers. He talks about responses to John the Baptist, a Jewish teacher who largely (but not exclusively) addressed Jews.

Is Jesus saying that actions count more than intentions? As we saw, Claire thought so and disagreed. In some ways, it would be surprising to find Jesus saying this. In a number of other passages, we see Jesus emphasising intention: he talks of murder and adultery 'in the heart' (see Chapter 8). Such sins can be committed by way of intention alone. Isn't there a contradiction between that teaching and this parable?

Sex workers in the kingdom of God   115

To find an answer to this question, it's worth noting that the first son is said to have changed his mind (or 'thought better of it') after saying no. But there is no reference to the second son changing his mind. The implication may be that he never intended to work in the vineyard. His promise was empty words.

Perhaps then Jesus was not contrasting actions with intentions. He was contrasting actions with words, with promises, with appearances. Or, as Pandora put it, with social acceptability.

Many commentators, after discussing these sorts of questions, quickly move on. This leaves another crucial question unasked – and, of course, unanswered. Why did Jesus mention tax collectors and sex workers specifically?

To answer this question, we need to think a bit more about who constituted these two groups of people.

The Roman Empire collected a great many taxes from its subjects. Some were gathered directly by the empire's agents. For other sorts of taxes, the Romans gave contracts to local businesspeople to collect the taxes for them. In today's language, this sort of tax collection was 'contracted out' or 'privatised'. The people who ran these tax-collecting businesses had to collect enough to make a profit and pay their workers as well as to hand over the required sums of money to the Romans. Some scholars use the translation 'toll collectors', because many of these taxes involved fees paid for entering a town or exporting goods.

These collectors had a reputation for being bullies. They were doing 'unclean' work, handling Roman coins (considered idolatrous by many devout Jews). They had taken employment with the occupying power. No wonder they were unpopular.

They were not, however, wealthy. The people at the head of tax-collecting businesses may have been wealthy: Luke's Gospel tells the story of one such person who repented and gave away half his wealth after meeting Jesus.[2] But most tax collectors were employees of such people. Recent scholarship suggests that 'most of the tax collectors who did the actual work were impoverished ... and quickly dismissed if problems arose'.[3]

The Upside-down Bible

There are people who tell me that we should not hate wealthy bankers because they are today's equivalent of tax collectors in first-century Palestine. Jesus discouraged hate and promoted love for all, including enemies, so I am sure he would not want us to hate bankers. In economic terms, however, they are likely to be as far from the tax collectors of the gospels as it is possible to be. The tax collectors included people in desperate poverty who took on insecure and unpopular work in order to survive.

This in turn gave them something in common with sex workers. As in most societies, the majority of sex workers were very poor. Elisabeth Schüssler Fiorenza, who specialises in studying women in New Testament times, explains, 'Prostitutes usually were slaves, daughters who had been sold or rented out by their husbands, poor women, exposed girls, the divorced and widowed, single mothers, captives of war or piracy, women bought for soldiers ... In Palestine, torn by war, colonial taxation and famine, the number of such women must have been great.'[4]

Pandora and Sarah, who were quoted above, are happy doing sex work. There are other sex workers, in our own society and others, who are not. Most sex workers in Jesus' society, like most tax collectors, had little or no choice about their work. Let's not forget that this would have been true for most people. Indeed, it is true for most people in today's world. Some who take work where they can get it can find themselves doing more disreputable work than others. In Jesus' society, it is doubtful if any work was more stigmatised than sex work and tax collection.

Thus the two groups of people whom Jesus mentions were both poor and socially excluded.

Should we then describe the sex workers and tax collectors of Jesus' day as more sinned against than sinning? I think we need to be cautious. There is a danger that we see them as passive victims. This is how many people view sex workers today and it is unlikely to do much to help them to tackle the injustices they face.

Was Jesus saying that *even* sex workers and tax collectors were going into the kingdom of God ahead of the Pharisees? Or did he mean that they *specifically* were right at the front? Jesus may have mentioned such groups because he realised the shock value of championing them. However, he also praised them for a particular action: listening to John the Baptist and putting their faith in his teachings.

Jesus was several times accused of associating with such people. It was known that John had baptised sex workers and several scholars argue that there were probably a fair number of them in Jesus' movement. This then leads on to an important but rarely asked question, the one that Sarah asked above. Did the sex workers and tax collectors give up being sex workers and tax collectors when they became followers of Jesus?

The evidence is mixed. On the one hand, the gospels tell of a tax collector who encountered Jesus and who is said to have immediately left his toll booth to follow him.[5] On the other hand, Jesus was accused of eating 'with tax collectors', not with *former* tax collectors. Scholars such as Luise Schottroff argue that many sex workers continued in their former work after joining Jesus' movement.

'Our own presuppositions ... dictate whether we think of these women as giving up prostitution or not,' writes William Countryman. 'There is nothing in Matthew's Gospel to settle the question.' He adds that sex workers who gave up their work, 'would have had only the most limited of options, since they would not have been acceptable as wives'.[6]

A possible answer lies in the nature of Jesus' community. For his closest followers, serving the kingdom of God seems to have meant rejecting other powers and systems, such as property, family and obedience to authority. At least some of his followers probably shared their possessions in common (see Chapter 6 for more on this). If the sex workers did give up their work, they may have survived by living from the common purse of the Jesus community. This possibility should not be overlooked.

Jesus' movement, however, began after the time of John

the Baptist. The sex workers baptised by John are therefore unlikely to have been able to support themselves if they did not continue selling sex. Thus Jesus not only praised people who were poor or stigmatised. He praised people whose lifestyles would be regarded by most Christians today as utterly immoral. They are the ones walking first into the kingdom of God.

QUESTIONS

1. Which matters more – intentions or actions?
2. Did the sex workers and tax collectors continue in their work after believing in John the Baptist and/or Jesus?
3. Who are the equivalent of the 'tax collectors and sex workers' in today's society?

NOTES

[1] John Chrysostom, cited by W. D. Davies and Dale C. Allison, *Matthew: A Shorter Commentary* (T&T Clark, 2004).
[2] Luke 19:2–10.
[3] Elisabeth Schüssler Fiorenza, *In Memory of Her: A Feminist Theological Reconstruction of Christian Origins* (SCM Press, 1983).
[4] Fiorenza, *In Memory of Her*.
[5] Matthew 9:9.
[6] William Countryman, *Dirt, Greed and Sex: Sexual Ethics in the New Testament and their Implications for Today* (SCM Press, 1988).

12. Love, sex and a dinner party

(Luke 7:36–50)

This is an account of Jesus' invitation to a meal. It can be found in Luke's Gospel (7:36–50), although a story with some similarities appears in the other gospels.

One of the Pharisees asked Jesus to eat with him, and he went into the Pharisee's house and took his place at the table. And a woman in the city, who was a sinner, having learned that he was eating in the Pharisee's house, brought an alabaster jar of ointment. She stood behind him at his feet, weeping, and began to bathe his feet with her tears and to dry them with her hair. Then she continued kissing his feet and anointing them with the ointment.

Language point

Pharisees: A Jewish religious and political group who emphasised strict adherence to the Jewish law.

Denarii: A unit of currency in the Roman Empire. One denarius was about a day's wages for a labourer.

Historical point

In the society in which Jesus lived, it was considered shocking for a respectable man to allow a woman to whom he was not married or related to make physical contact with him.

Now when the Pharisee who had invited him saw it, he said to himself, 'If this man were a prophet, he would have known who and what kind of woman this is who is touching him – that she is a sinner.'

Jesus spoke up and said to him, 'Simon, I have something to say to you.'

'Teacher,' he replied, 'speak.'

'A certain creditor had two debtors; one owed five hundred denarii, and the other fifty. When they could not pay, he cancelled the debts for both of them. Now which of them will love him more?'

Simon answered, 'I suppose the one for whom he cancelled the greater debt.'

And Jesus said to him, 'You have judged rightly.'

Then turning towards the woman, he said to Simon, 'Do you see this woman? I entered your house; you gave me no water for my feet, but she has bathed my feet with her tears and dried them with her hair. You gave me no kiss, but from the time I came in she has not stopped kissing my feet. You did not anoint my head with oil, but she has anointed my feet with ointment. Therefore, I tell you, her sins, which were many, have been forgiven; hence she has shown great love. But the one to whom little is forgiven, loves little.'

Then he said to her, 'Your sins are forgiven.'

But those who were at the table with him began to say among themselves, 'Who is this who even forgives sins?'

And he said to the woman, 'Your faith has saved you; go in peace.'[1]

REACTIONS

What are your initial reactions to this story? Luke describes the woman in Simon's house as a 'sinner'. Would your reaction be different if this phrase was not included?

INSIGHTS

'It is pretty kinky, isn't it?'

This was one of the first responses to this passage when I led a workshop on Christianity in a fetish club. We were looking at some Bible passages about sexuality and gender. This passage drew the interest of several people with foot fetishes. But most found the story rather confusing. Someone described it as 'weird'.

This is not surprising. Many people, including lots of Christians, find this story confusing. First-time readers responded with comments such as 'It threw me', 'I don't understand anything about it at all' and 'The more I read it, the more it annoys me'.

The first comment from Heather was, 'I actually wondered how the woman had got into Simon's house.' Samantha asked, 'Where would we be if we had to cry over our friend's feet every time we went round?'

Jennifer, whose hair is so long that it reaches to the top of her legs, wondered 'what it would take' for her to use her hair in the way that the woman in this story did with Jesus.

Frederik said he was 'in two minds' about the story. He explained, 'On the one hand it seems as if Jesus' forgiveness meant a lot to the woman and made her happy, so that is quite heart-warming.' But on the other hand, 'I wonder if he really addressed the root cause of her distress, or just gave her some superficial feeling of relief that won't last very long.'

'I thought she was a bit obsequious,' said Dunyazade. Jennifer said that the word 'sinner' is the only description this woman has. For Heather, the use of that word makes the story more 'sexualised'. Sally said, 'This description is just plonked on her and we are supposed to believe it.'

She added, 'My reaction is that she's either done something

really trivial that they class as "sin" because of their warped religious beliefs, or that she's done something that I wouldn't see as sinful. I think my assumption is that she is probably a prostitute and I don't think prostitutes are "sinners".'

Samantha, who is a Pagan, said, 'Reading between the lines I am going to assume she's some manner of sex worker. I did wonder if she might not be a perfectly happy sacred temple whore for some fabulous ancient goddess, but I suppose she wouldn't be crying on Jesus' feet if she were.'

Nonetheless, Samantha was largely positive about Jesus' behaviour. She said, 'It is clearly a double shocker that Jesus is letting firstly a woman he's not married to, and secondly a sinner, even touch him, let alone cry on his feet and so on.' In the workshop at the fetish event, there was a positive response to the idea that Jesus accepted a form of consensual physical intimacy that would have shocked those around him.

Dunyazade, however, thought that the woman's action should not be seen as sexual. 'I don't think she was doing anything particularly shocking,' she explained. Dunyazade said that the interaction between Jesus and the woman was not one of equals. She added, 'Maybe that would have been more shocking, if it had been on an equal basis.'

Jesus' apparent lack of conversation with the woman also concerned others. 'I would question him for not going to her aid,' said Louise. 'If a woman is crying, you wouldn't just let her kiss your feet, you'd try to console her.' Given the intimacy of the woman's actions, Jennifer wondered why Jesus seemed to think that 'talking to the man is more important'.

Was Jesus challenging the values of those around him? Sally said that Jesus had not challenged popular perceptions about women's sexuality. She explained, 'Jesus still believes she has sinned, but he chooses to forgive her. He doesn't argue against the codes which say women and men can't touch.'

Samantha, on the other hand, said, 'Jesus is, I think, doing a good thing, if not a God thing.' She suggested that Simon and the others 'are "slut-shaming" the woman, by calling her a sinner', but that Jesus' attitude challenges this. However, she added that the idea of someone needing forgiveness from Jesus 'sits uncomfortably' with her.

Others were also disturbed by Jesus' comments. Frederik said that Jesus' words reminded him of 'how some emotionally abusive men and women will lower their partners' self-esteem to make them needy of the abuser's "love"'.

Louise took a similar view. Describing Jesus as 'manipulative', she insisted that his behaviour 'is not kindness, it is thinly veiled abuse'.

REFLECTION

This is a strange story. It defies all attempts to categorise it. No interpretation that I have read, however helpful, has quite managed to explain the whole thing. There are bits left around the edges that will just not fit into the neat interpretations that many commentators like to come up with. It's an awkward story that won't do what we want it to.

Many of our first-time readers found it weird, alien, inexplicable. Paradoxically, they nearly all had lots to say about it. I've been struggling with this passage for years yet keep finding new angles on it – or others find them for me, as new conversations raise points I had never thought about.

All four gospels tell of a woman anointing Jesus with oil. In John's Gospel, a woman called Mary of Bethany spontaneously washes Jesus' feet with expensive oil.[2] In Mark and Matthew, an unnamed woman surprises Jesus' companions by chucking oil over his head.[3] There may have been only one incident that's turned into several stories. More likely, several incidents have got mixed up. In any case, all four stories are somewhat bizarre, but Luke's is the most puzzling of all.

Part of the oddness lies in the differences between our own culture and the one in which Jesus lived. But this does not explain it all. The incident and the conversation around it may well have seemed just as disturbing to the guests in the Pharisee's house as to us.

Above, we saw Heather wondering how the woman had got into the house. It seems unlikely that Simon the Pharisee would have invited a woman associated with sin. Some commentators go into great detail about the layout of Palestinian houses in the first century, and the tendency to leave the doors open. In Luke's Gospel, Jesus frequently teaches and discusses controversial issues while eating in someone else's house. New Testament scholar Deirdre Good writes that Luke's early readers would 'recognise this kind of meal as a symposium, a philosophical discourse that takes place in a dining room'. Such events, says Good, were 'semi-public'.[4]

While this might explain how the woman entered the room, it doesn't make the meaning of her behaviour any clearer. A number of religious teachers of the time avoided associating with women in public. By allowing a 'sinful' woman to touch him, Jesus was flouting the Jewish purity laws.[5] It is hard to know how well such purity laws were observed in practice, but the Pharisees were keen on them and Simon would have expected a religious teacher, let alone a 'prophet', to uphold them. There is no reason to think that Jesus and the woman regarded their behaviour as sexual, but their observers probably did.

There are several occasions in the gospels on which Jesus is shown making physical contact with a woman, often with a reference to the shock of those nearby. In every case, it is the woman, rather than Jesus, who initiates the contact, but Jesus accepts it.

Why had Simon invited Jesus? He doesn't seem to have been very hospitable. Jesus said that Simon did not give him water for his feet or kiss him when he arrived. To us, this might make Jesus sound like a prima donna, but Middle Eastern commentators suggest that Simon had not observed the basic rules of hospitality in his culture. Being able to wash the sand and dust from your feet was important. Perhaps Simon never really thought that Jesus was a prophet and had invited him for the purpose of catching him out.

If you hear a sermon about this passage, there's a good chance that it will involve a number of assumptions. Samantha and Sally both suspected that the woman was a sex worker, although neither was definite about it. In contrast, a good many commentators and preachers simply assert that this was the case. The common interpretation is that she repented of her profession and, overcome with remorse, came to beg for Jesus' forgiveness. As a result of receiving it, she showed great love.

This superficially neat explanation leaves many questions unanswered. As some of our first-time readers asked, why did Jesus not react to the woman sooner? Why did he not let her touch him as an equal? How did he know what she was repenting of? Furthermore, why should we assume she was a sex worker? And how would she now support herself if she had given up her work?

Any attempt to answer these questions involves speculation if not guesswork. There is nothing wrong with speculating, as long as we recognise that this is what we are doing. It's when we state our speculations or assumptions as fact that we have gone too far.

Scholars have offered several explanations that may go some distance to explaining the confusing parts of this story – but not all the way.

Let's take the question of why Jesus did not speak to the woman sooner. Should he have encouraged her to stand up straight away? Or knelt down on the floor where she was? In another incident recorded in John's Gospel, Jesus was sufficiently humble to get down on his knees, pick up a towel and wash the feet of his own disciples.[6]

Sally was disappointed that Jesus didn't 'argue against the codes which say women and men can't touch'. It could be said that Jesus challenged such codes implicitly by allowing the woman to touch him, thus he did not need to make a verbal argument. In this story, people communicate at least as much by actions as by words. But should Jesus have gone further in his comments?

As far as Luke tells us, Jesus didn't speak to the woman until after he had finished arguing with Simon. It may be that Jesus *did* speak to the woman, but that Luke – or other people who told the story before him – did not think that this part of the narrative was important, so it got missed out. In this case, the blame for the

The Upside-down Bible

sexism goes to Luke or his predecessors rather than Jesus. Luke has been accused by feminist scholars of portraying women largely in passive roles; more so than the other gospels.

Another answer might be that Jesus did not speak to the woman at first because it was Simon he wanted to challenge. If Jesus was concerned with challenging the powerful and siding with the marginalised, this could lead paradoxically to stories in which he appears to ignore the marginalised because he was talking to the powerful.

Perhaps the most satisfying explanation is that Jesus and the woman had met before. There is no reason to assume that they did not know each other.

Ibn al-Tayyib, a Christian scholar in Baghdad in the eleventh century, thought it likely that the two of them had met previously and that the woman was turning up to show her gratitude for forgiveness she had already received. Al-Tayyib even suggested that Jesus accepted Simon's invitation in the hope of encouraging the Pharisees to acknowledge the woman's repentance.[7]

Do any of these suggestions sound convincing to you? Or do they fail to give a persuasive explanation of why we don't see Jesus talking with the woman sooner?

What if she was a sex worker? What if she wasn't? Does it matter? Sex work would certainly have gained her a poor reputation and the Pharisees' disapproval. Some scholars argue that only a sex worker would let her hair run loose in that culture. Others have challenged the historical accuracy of this claim.[8] In any case, the woman and Jesus were already breaking social codes to such an extent that one more should hardly be taken as evidence of a scandalous profession!

Perhaps we are too influenced by common assumptions about women's sexuality. If a woman is described as a sinner, we assume her sin is sexual. Biblical scholar Barbara Reid suggests that readers can easily display the same sort of prejudices as the Pharisee and 'reinforce Simon's initial perception' when we encounter this woman.[9]

Not all feminist readers reject the idea that the woman

was a sex worker. Luise Schottroff, a prominent New Testament scholar, argues that the woman *was* a sex worker – but that it wasn't her sex work of which she was repenting. Several Bible passages suggest that Jesus' followers included sex workers and Schottroff insists that they provide no basis for the belief that such women had to repent of their profession. 'The texts show that women provide for themselves by means of the sex trade, since that is the only way open to them to survive,' she says, adding that these sex workers looked for 'solidarity' in Jesus' movement.[10] (See Chapter 11 for more on this.)

This interpretation makes Jesus' behaviour even more shocking: he was not offering forgiveness to someone who *had* worked in the sex trade, but to someone who *still did*.

Whether or not the woman was a sex worker, of what was she repenting if not of sex work? There are as many answers as there are sins. Most people would acknowledge that they have at times behaved selfishly or immorally, and it may be that the woman was no more or less sinful than most of us – even if her behaviour meant that her sins were known about.

Andre Trocme was a French theologian and activist who emphasised the revolutionary nature of love. He wrote, 'We do not know the nature of the woman's love for Jesus. Did she recognise him as the Messiah, the Son of God who was capable of purifying her? Or was she simply overwhelmed upon meeting for the first time a genuinely pure man who treated her like a sister or a friend?'[11]

In the middle of this passage is a parable that Jesus told to Simon: the parable of the two debtors. Very few commentators remark on the fact that the parable is, on one level, about money. Churches are often keen to turn Jesus' teachings about money into metaphors for something else, to avoid addressing economic issues (as we saw in Chapters 3 and 4).

In this case, however, such an approach might seem justified, for the conversation moves straight back to the woman's sin. But why choose a monetary parable? What if the woman's sin had something to do with money? Perhaps she had refused to cancel a debt but had since repented of her harshness? Perhaps she had *literally* had a debt cancelled and this was one reason for her gratitude. This is, of course, only my guesswork. The role of money in the story is unclear.

Before we leave the subject, let's have a look at the sums of money Jesus mentioned. One person owes fifty denarrii, another five hundred denarii. The smaller debt is not small. Fifty denarrii was over two months' wages for a labourer. If the two debtors represent Simon and the woman at Jesus' feet, it seems Jesus regards Simon as more sinful than he would like to think.

Above, we saw Louise and Frederik suggesting that Jesus was being manipulative towards a distraught woman as he talked of love and forgiveness. I believe this point needs to be taken seriously. It is quite possible to talk of such things in a way that exploits someone's emotions, especially someone in a vulnerable state.

Perhaps Jesus' words take on a different light if we read them as addressed to Simon and his dinner guests rather than to the woman. Simon, it seems, did not recognise his own sins – including his judgemental attitude towards this woman. Perhaps it was not that his sins were less than hers, but rather that he recognised them less. He thought he had little need for forgiveness, so displayed little love. The woman, on the other hand, had recognised her sins and repented. By this reading, Jesus was not forgiving her at that moment, but rather affirming that her sins had already been forgiven.

Ibn al-Tayyib said that the story was not about one great sinner, but two. Biblical scholar Kenneth Bailey writes, 'The judge (Simon) becomes the accused. The drama begins with Jesus under scrutiny. The tables turn and Simon is exposed.'[12]

Does this make us more comfortable with this story? If it does, should it? Jesus' life and teachings were disturbing. It is better to wrestle amidst confusion than to pretend we have all the answers.

One line in this passage is rarely mentioned. Barbara Reid regards it as the most important element of the whole story. Jesus asked Simon, 'Do you see this woman?' On one level, it's a comical question. Simon could hardly have failed to notice her. But if we believe that Jesus is on the woman's side, the question takes on a new meaning. Simon has seen only a sinner. Jesus, we hope, has seen first and foremost a human being. Large numbers of people are still written off by society and by religious institutions, demeaned and ignored because of their poverty, their sexuality, their work or their reputation. Do we see them?

QUESTIONS

1. In the light of these varied interpretations, what do you now make of the woman? Was she a sex worker? Of what was she repenting?

2. Would you have liked Jesus to behave differently to how he did?

3. Who might be the Pharisee and the woman in our own society?

NOTES

1   This translation is from the New Revised Standard Version (Anglicized edition).
2   John 12:3–8.
3   Mark 14:3–9.
4   Deirdre Good, *Jesus' Family Values* (Seabury Books, 2006).
5   William Countryman, *Dirt, Greed and Sex: Sexual Ethics in the New Testament and their Implications for Today* (SCM Press, 1988).
6   John 13:4–5.
7   Cited by Kenneth E. Bailey, *Through Peasant Eyes: A Literary-critical Approach to the Parables in Luke* (William B Eerdmans, 1980).
8   Teresa J. Hornsby, 'The Woman is a Sinner/The Sinner is a Woman' in *A Feminist Companion to Luke*, ed. Amy-Jill Levine with Marianne Blickenstaff (Sheffield Academic Press, 2002).
9   Barbara E. Reid, 'Do you see this woman?' in *A Feminist Companion to Luke*, ed. Levine with Blickenstaff (Sheffield Academic Press, 2002).
10 Luise Schottroff, Silvia Schroer and Marie-Theres Wacker, *Feminist Interpretation: The Bible in Women's Perspective* (Augsburg Fortress, 1998).
11 Andre Trocme, *Jesus and the Nonviolent Revolution* (Plough Publishing House, 2003 [1973]), trans. Martin H. Shank and Martin E. Miller.
12 Bailey, *Through Peasant Eyes.*

Part Three. Violence

13. Hate crimes and hospitality

(Luke 10:25–37)

This story appears in Luke's Gospel (10:25–37)

And now a lawyer stood up and, to test Jesus, asked, 'Master, what must I do to inherit eternal life?'

He said to him, 'What is written in the Law? What is your reading of it?'

He replied, 'You must love the Lord your God with all your heart, with all your soul, with all your strength and with all your mind, and your neighbour as yourself.'

Jesus said to him, 'You have answered right, do this and life is yours.'

Language point

Samaritans: Generally speaking, residents of Samaria, an area of Palestine. In religious terms, they had certain beliefs and practices in common with Jews but disagreed strongly in other areas. Jews and Samaritans often regarded each other as enemies.

Levites: A hereditary group with ceremonial and practical duties within Jewish religion and worship.

Denarii: A currency in the Roman Empire. At this time, one denarius was about a day's wages for a labourer.

But the man was anxious to justify himself and said to Jesus, 'And who is my neighbour?'

In answer Jesus said, 'A man was once on his way down from Jerusalem to Jericho and fell into the hands of bandits; they stripped him, beat him, and then made off, leaving him half dead. Now a priest happened to be travelling down the same road, but when he saw the man, he passed by on the other side. In the same way a Levite who came to the place saw him, and passed by on the other side.

'But a Samaritan traveller who came on him was moved with compassion when he saw him. He went up to him and bandaged his wounds, pouring oil and wine on them. He then lifted him on his own mount and took him to an inn and looked after him. Next day he took out two denarii and handed them to the innkeeper, and said, 'Look after him, and on my way back I will make good any extra expense you have'.

'Which of these three, do you think, proved himself a neighbour to the man who fell into the bandits' hands?'

He replied, 'The one who showed pity towards him.'

Jesus said to him, 'Go, and do the same yourself.'

REACTIONS

With which character(s) in this story do you find it easiest to identify? How often have you heard this story before? If you're familiar with it, did anything new strike you as you read it through?

INSIGHTS

This is perhaps the most well-known story in the New Testament. Most people in Britain have heard the phrase 'Good Samaritan', although many may not know the details or be aware that it derives from a story told by Jesus.

I went on social media to find out some of the reactions that are triggered by the words 'Good Samaritan'. What, I asked, comes into your mind when you hear the words? I quickly received replies from both Christians and non-Christians.

'Primary school assemblies' was the answer from several people. One remembered, 'Images from children's illustrated Bibles of cartoon men dressed in long, beige, flowing robes stood on the side of a dusty road'. Another replied, 'A man lying injured on the road, with bushes nearby. An inn not too far away with palm trees.'

Some comments suggested a half-remembered story. Somebody wrote, 'An image in my head of two men on a road. Followed by an image of the Samaritan with the other chap back in the Samaritan's lodgings so the other chap can rest. Not sure if the latter part is accurate but that's what comes to mind.'

For others, the phrase meant 'somebody being unexpectedly nice' or 'a selfless act of kindness'. Several people said that the term made them think of the charity called the Samaritans, which provides a helpline service to people in distress. Some mentioned acts of kindness they had personally experienced and one said, 'I think there are plenty of examples of good Samaritans in our society, which makes me happy.'

Not everyone found the term positive. Four people went for the term 'do-gooder' and one linked it with 'paternalism'. Another said that the phrase 'reminds me of abusive ex, when he told me my big fault was that I "couldn't look the other way"'.

A few responses referred directly to the content of the parable. 'A challenge to all forms of racism,' said one person. Another wrote, 'The good Samaritan puts himself out to help the vulnerable, unknown stranger. He may not be "respectable" but he *is* righteous.' Someone else felt the term was usually

Hate crimes and hospitality

wrongly applied: 'Every time a stranger goes to help another person they are described as a Good Samaritan. That isn't the point of the parable!'

I asked a few people from different religious backgrounds to read through the passage and give me their reactions.

'In Judaism in general, there's a commandment to be there for people,' said Alice, a Jew. She suggested that the priest in particular would have been expected to help.

Nonetheless, she had some concerns about the story. She suggested that 'people might not "cross the road" if they feel they have to do all that the Samaritan does'.

On the other hand, she said, 'It's relatively easy to take care of the person in front of you, it's relatively easy to feel upset about an individual.' She said it was much harder to act when our neighbours are people whom we don't know, who may be on the other side of the world.

'It seems to me the whole passage is about the definition of "neighbour",' said Beccy, another Jew. She said that the Jewish relationship with God is special precisely because Jews are called to be 'a light unto the nations'. She compared the Samaritan with Israeli Jews today who support Palestinian human rights and who deliberately travel into the Occupied Palestinian Territories to show solidarity.

Angie, who is not religious, liked what she saw as the parable's message: that despite any differences between people 'it's important to try to look after and care for someone else in the way that you would want to be looked after'. She hoped that she would act like the Samaritan but added, 'I think that there might be a little of both the Samaritan and the priest in every human.'

But Angie was concerned that the story was told in response to a question about how to inherit eternal life. 'It's a shame that there has to be a "bribe" to behave kindly and in a thoughtful manner towards others,' she said. 'Is it not reward enough to know that you made another human being feel better?'

Fatimah, a Muslim, found that 'What really speaks to me in this passage is the emphasis on Love.' She said that loving God

The Upside-down Bible

and loving humanity as yourself 'is for me the essence of true faith whatever name it may carry'. She added, 'Some people of faith believe that only their brothers and sisters in their faith are their neighbours, which as this parable clearly shows, was not Jesus' belief on the matter'.

Fatimah concluded, 'Eternal life comes to those who love.'

REFLECTION

It's no wonder that this story has been popular for so long. Unlike some of the other passages we have looked at, you could know little or nothing about the historical background and still get something out of it. At the bare minimum, it is a story about kindness. Once we realise that Jews and Samaritans saw each other as enemies, the story takes on an additional dimension. And the more we read it, the more meanings tend to spring out. Are they all valid ones, or do we need to choose between them?

At school, I took the story as an instruction to be nice to people. As moral messages go, that's not a bad one. But the story goes so much further.

We begin with a lawyer's question. Jesus, never known for giving direct answers, responds with other questions.

Angie was disappointed that compassion is encouraged as an apparent route to eternal life. I can understand her concern. At the same time, there is a strong case to be made that this is not what Jesus is saying. The lawyer wants straightforward instructions, but he is instead told a story. Ibn al-Tayyib, an eleventh-century Baghdadi Christian, suggested that Jesus' indirect response was a refusal to accept the lawyer's premises. After all, he was trying to 'justify himself', to make himself look good. We should not ask how to inherit eternal life, but how to love. Paradoxically, as Fatimah said, eternal life comes to those who love.

The lawyer wants to know who his neighbour is. Although the term translated 'neighbour' is used in varied ways in different parts of the Jewish scriptures, it was generally taken to mean a fellow Jew. The Torah, or Law of Moses, encouraged Jews to treat non-Jews well, and to treat foreigners living among them with as much love as fellow Jews. But 'neighbour' generally meant other Jews. James Moffatt, who produced one of the twentieth century's first English translations of the Bible, rendered the word as 'fellow countryman'.[1] John Henson, in a more recent translation, uses the term 'the person next to you'.[2]

The New Testament scholar Kenneth Bailey suggests that Jesus does not really answer the question 'Who is my neighbour?' His story is an answer to a better question: 'To whom must I *become* a neighbour?'[3]

Two thousand years after Jesus, with a very different language and vastly different culture, we still tell stories based around three characters. We have the Three Little Pigs and the Three Bears. We have jokes about an Englishman, an Irishman and a Scotsman. The usual format is that the first two behave predictably but the third does something different. There were similar formats in Jesus' culture. Several scholars point to narratives that involve first a priest, then a Levite, then an Israelite (that is, a Jew who was not a priest or a Levite). So after the first two appear, the audience is expecting an Israelite. Instead, Jesus presents them with a Samaritan.

This is roughly the equivalent of listening to the story of the Three Bears and finding that after Daddy Bear and Mummy Bear, we meet not Baby Bear, but a snake.

There are several accounts from the time of acts of violence between Jews and Samaritans: Jewish travellers attacked or killed while going through Samaria, Jews attacking Samaritans in return. Some of these were individual assaults – what we would now call 'hate crimes'. At times, things got more heated and involved large numbers of people.

It seems that Jesus is effectively telling the lawyer to become a neighbour to his enemies. By holding up an apparent enemy – a Samaritan – as someone who did this, Jesus makes clear that the people we look down on may be the very people from whom we have most to learn.

Sometimes when this story is told, this message is overlaid with anti-Jewish prejudice. It is suggested that the priest and Levite were more concerned with religious ritual than with compassion. Some scholars say that they were concerned about the danger of breaking ritual purity laws. However, as Alice said, Jewish law *required* not just priests and Levites but other Jews to help someone who was wounded (whether or not the wounded person was Jewish). Amy-Jill Levine, a Jewish scholar of the New Testament, makes a similar point.[4] It is bitterly ironic that a story that challenges racial prejudice has been used to fuel it.

If we want to blame the priest and the Levite's behaviour on Judaism, perhaps it's because we are reluctant to admit how likely we are to act like them. I imagine myself walking through dark streets late at night in a city I don't know. I'm nervous, cold and want to get back to where I'm staying. I see a man lying in the road. Should I do something? He's probably drunk. It's probably his fault. I probably can't do anything anyway. I think I'll carry on.

And that's before I even know whether the person is racially, politically or religiously different to me.

In other words, I like to think that I would act like the Samaritan but fear I would behave like the priest. If asked, 'With which character do you identify?', there is another possible answer: the wounded man. It's odd how rarely we discuss things from his perspective. Yet here he is, being helped by someone he has learnt to fear and possibly hate. Is this story about offering compassion *to* our enemies? Or about being willing to accept hospitality *from* them? Could the latter be even harder than the former?

In modern society, we are often encouraged to feel shame about being 'dependent' on someone else. Those who need to turn to the welfare state are routinely demonised in parts of the press. The reality is that no one is independent. When I cook a meal, I rely on thousands of people who have grown, packaged, transported and sold the food. In this context, one way to read this parable is an encouragement to be willing to accept hospitality from others, and to recognise our mutual dependence.

As Beccy said, an equivalent story could be told to almost any group of people. In Samaria, someone might have told a story about a compassionate Jew. In the western world today, we might want to tell the story of the 'Good Muslim'. In the 1980s, a British Christian drama group produced an update of this parable in which a vicar and a social worker ignore an injured man who is then helped by a punk rocker (remember them?). Variations on this theme can be used to challenge liberals as well as traditionalists. A left-wing group could be told a story about a wounded person helped by a Conservative politician after being ignored by a vegan chef and a *Guardian* journalist.

It's a sign of the parable's strength that it can produce such re-tellings, and there is something to be said for them. But for some, they do not go nearly far enough. A number of Christian anti-racist campaigners are keen to emphasise that this is a story about race. James Cone, who pioneered the 'black theology' movement in the USA from the 1960s, reads the story as a rejection of racism. Another theologian, J. Denny Weaver, insists that the parable is a reminder that participation in the kingdom of God 'calls for racial and ethnic reconciliation'. He adds, 'Jesus' transcending of barriers between Jews and Samaritans makes visible this reconciliation.'[5]

If we re-tell this story in a variety of ways, do we risk watering down its emphasis on race? Or can we adapt it to fit the audience, without undermining its anti-racist message? It's a question we might want to bear in mind if we are trying to produce modern rewritings of the story.

In 2015, shortly after a racist massacre in a church in South Carolina, the writer John Metta preached a sermon in Washington State. He said, 'If I could rewrite that story, I'd rewrite it from the perspective of Black America. What if the person wasn't beaten and bloody? What if it wasn't so obvious? What if they were just systematically challenged in a thousand small ways that actually made it easier for *you* to succeed in life?'[6]

Beccy suggested that the story is about the definition of 'neighbour'. Jesus took a word that applied to people living in the same country and applied it not only to foreigners but to a group of which his audience were likely to be frightened. Can this challenge nationalism as well as racism? Can we see someone on the other side of the world as our neighbour? Someone fighting against our government's armed forces as our neighbour? Can we love them on the grounds that they are *just as much our neighbours* as those who share our faith and speak our language?

It's easy to say that Christians believe in doing this. I am reminded of how much Christian groups in Britain publicise the persecution of Christians elsewhere in the world. It is right that we care for persecuted Christians and speak out about it. But why only persecuted Christians? Does the parable of the surprising Samaritan not suggest that we should care just as much about persecuted Muslims, persecuted Hindus and persecuted atheists?

This story is about race and it's about violence. Let's look again at how it ends. As we saw above, one of the people who responded to me on social media had 'an image of the Samaritan with the other chap back in the Samaritan's lodgings so the other chap can rest'. Delightful though this image is, the parable's ending is far scarier. The Samaritan took the wounded man to an inn. Perhaps it was in Jericho, perhaps a village. A Samaritan rides into a *Jewish town* with a half-dead Jew. What are people likely to think? Who's in danger now? Perhaps the Samaritan is a reminder of the risks we may be called to take to resist violence and racism.

Martin Luther King quoted the parable of the Good Samaritan in a speech in 1968. He said the Samaritan had taken risks because he feared what would happen to the wounded man if he had not. This motivated King to continue his work, despite death threats, because of what would happen if he gave it up.

The next day, Martin Luther King was assassinated.

QUESTIONS

1. Is this parable primarily a story about race? About violence? About prejudice? Do we have to choose?
2. Is it really possible to regard everyone as your neighbour? What does this mean in practice?
3. What risks are you willing and able – or unwilling or unable – to take for the sake of compassion and justice

---

NOTES

1 James Moffatt, *A New Translation of the Bible* (Hodder & Stoughton, 1950).
2 John Henson, *Good as New: A Radical Retelling of the Scriptures* (O Books, 2004).
3 Kenneth E. Bailey, *Jesus through Middle Eastern Eyes: Cultural Studies in the Gospels* (SPCK, 2008).
4 Amy-Jill Levine, *Short Stories by Jesus: The Enigmatic Parables of a Controversial Rabbi* (HarperCollins, 2014).
5 J. Denny Weaver, *The Nonviolent God* (William B. Eerdmans, 2013).
6 John Metta, 'I, racist' in *Huffington Post*, 10 July 2015.

14. The men caught in hypocrisy

(John 8:2–11)

This account can be found in the Gospel of John.

At daybreak, Jesus appeared in the Temple again; and as all the people came to him, he sat down and began to teach them.

The scribes and Pharisees brought a woman along who had been caught committing adultery; and making her stand there in the middle, they said to Jesus, 'Master, this woman was caught in the very act of committing adultery, and in the Law, Moses ordered us to stone women of this kind. What have you got to say?'

They asked him this as a test, looking for an accusation to use against him.

But Jesus bent down and started writing on the ground with his finger.

As they persisted with their question, he straightened up and said, 'Let the one among you who is guiltless be the first to throw a stone at her.' Then he bent down and continued writing on the ground.

When they heard this, they went away one by one, beginning with the eldest, until the last one had gone and Jesus was left alone with the woman, who remained in the middle.

Jesus again straightened up and said, 'Woman, where are they? Has no one condemned you?'

'No one, sir,' she replied.

'Neither do I condemn you,' said Jesus. 'Go away, and from this moment sin no more.'

REACTIONS

How do you react to this story? Would your reaction be different if the person concerned had been accused of a different crime rather than adultery?

INSIGHTS

'This was my favourite story,' said Samantha after reading several of the passages that appear in this book. 'It might be because Jesus is sticking up for a woman.'

Samantha liked the Jesus she found here. She explained, 'Sometimes in the other stories I felt he was unhelpfully aggressive and elusive, but this time he seemed mellower, and I wonder if that's because he's being gentle for this frightened woman's sake.'

Jennifer was also struck by Jesus' manner. 'Jesus is very calm,' she said. 'His calm demeanour has power.'

Heather suggested that Jesus 'recognises that everyone is a sinner, even himself, as he will not throw a stone either'.

Frederik had a mixed response to Jesus' attitude. He said that Jesus 'kept an innocent woman from being murdered, which is great'. But he added that Jesus 'doesn't react like a modern person – he clearly considers what she has done a "sin", without enquiring why she did it'.

Sally was fairly critical. She said, 'I think Jesus is still quite judgemental of the woman.' She explained, 'He does not ask her to tell him her side of the story, but just assumes that what the men have told him is correct.'

Heather thought that Jesus 'comes across as rather paternal towards the woman'.

Dunyazade thought that the story was about 'not judging people'. She added that this is also an important principle in her own religion, Islam. 'Yes, people do sin,' she said, 'but you're not supposed to be looking out for their sins.'

In similar vein, Adam, who does not practise a religion, said that the principle he found in the story 'has always represented a core tenet of morality for me'. He explained, 'We should be slow to judge others, we should remember that we all make mistakes, get things wrong.'

Heather said, 'There is no explanation of why Jesus is writing on the ground, although this is probably totally insignificant to the story!'

But Samantha found that 'The writing on the ground gave him a personality for me. It seemed like a mystical move, like he was consulting something or seeking guidance, and also shutting out these people.'

Jess said, 'I'm confused by the bit about "testing" him.' It was the first passage Jess read for this book, whereas Samantha had by now become familiar with stories about people 'testing' Jesus. She said, 'I felt that he was bored of these stupid people asking him questions and trying to catch him out, as though he feels they're missing the point he's trying to make entirely.'

Jennifer suggested that Jesus' 'calm reason' gave him power in the situation. She added, 'My first thought was that Jesus' calmness scared the Scribes but that doesn't make sense. Or does it? He makes them consider their actions and that's pretty scary.'

However, if Jesus' answer was based on avoiding a trap, then it weakened his words for Dunyazade. 'It feels that it takes away the moral of the actual story,' she explained.

The first thing that struck Sally was that 'it was the woman who the Scribes and Pharisees wanted to punish, not the man she supposedly committed adultery with, or both of them. Why was it seen as her sin and not his?'

Heather asked, 'Is the implication that all women are sinners?'

Samantha thought Jesus was challenging prejudiced attitudes to women. She said, 'Jesus appears to me to equate all sin and all sinners equally in this story – regardless of gender.'

Would Jesus have reacted in the same way if the person concerned had been accused of something else rather than adultery? Should he have done?

'I think he would have reacted a similar way to a different crime,' said Jess, as Jesus was 'all about forgiving people'.

Adam was unsure if he would want Jesus to behave the same way regardless of the crime. He said, 'I'd never want someone to be stoned to death, so saving someone from that would always seem to me to be the right thing to do.' But he added, 'An absolute refusal to condemn bad behaviours would be a worrying principle on its own. Sometimes, you need to say that something is wrong.'

REFLECTION

Adultery was regarded as a serious crime in first-century Palestine. It is highly unlikely that any Jewish teacher of the time, Jesus included, would have treated it as a trivial matter. Nor would his listeners or the early readers of this story.

The Upside-down Bible

This is precisely what makes Jesus' attitude so shocking.

Most readers today have a positive response to Jesus in this story. Commentators and church leaders throughout history have also been full of praise for his behaviour. In many cases, however, they have been quick to qualify their comments. The influential sixteenth-century theologian John Calvin asked if Jesus' statement about the guiltless throwing stones was 'driving all witnesses from the witness box and all judges from their bench'. His answer was that Jesus was not saying that sinners could never judge sinners. Instead he was criticising hypocrites who don't acknowledge their own sins and are 'savage judges of others'.[1]

It's easy to see how this interpretation would make sense for Calvin, who advocated relatively humane punishments in the context of his day but who wasn't going to let people off serious crimes. This attitude continues. Raymond Brown, one of the twentieth century's most prominent commentators on John's Gospel, insisted that 'One should beware of attempts to make it a general norm forbidding enactment of capital punishment'.[2]

These sort of comments sound suspiciously as if they are encouraging us to admire Jesus but not to follow his example. However, it *is* the case that Jesus emphasised intentions and motives as well as consequences. In many ways, this is one of the most distinctive things about his teachings. For example, he suggested that someone can commit murder or adultery in their heart as well as in their actions (see Chapter 8).[3] Against this, it can be argued that focusing on the Pharisees' *intentions* stops us from applying Jesus' teaching more widely (a similar issue came up in Chapter 5, when we looked at Jesus' comments about rich people entering the kingdom of God).

Perhaps a look at the context of the story will help us to sort this out?

Here we encounter a problem. Although this passage appears in John's Gospel, it was not originally part of it. The earliest manuscripts do not include it at all and it is written in

The men caught in hypocrisy

a different style to the rest of John. Nearly all scholars believe that it was added at a later date. Some believe that it is a later, inauthentic story but most scholars think it more likely that the story had circulated for a long time, either orally or as part of a longer document that is now lost.

If only we had that document, we could see what Jesus is said to have done before or after this incident. Its absence makes our task more difficult.

Things are complicated further by what looks at first like an unlikely scenario. If this woman had been sentenced to death by a court, why would anyone bring her to a controversial preacher such as Jesus to ask him to rule on the matter? It's hardly as if he were likely to have the power to stop the execution. Palestine was then part of the Roman Empire and the Romans gave the Jews only limited authority in the administration of domestic matters. It seems likely that by this time, this did not include the power to impose the death penalty.

The story might make more sense if we follow Raymond Brown's suggestion that it is more about a lynch mob than a judicial process.[4] Perhaps these people discovered the woman and resolved to carry out 'justice' themselves.

The first-time readers quoted above provide us with an insight. Samantha picked up on the point that Jesus was being 'tested'. In other words, the Scribes and Pharisees brought this woman to him to try to trick or trap him, or at least to see if he would uphold the law. Biblical scholar Kenneth Bailey suggests that they were disturbed by Jesus' challenge to their authority and thought that his popularity would fade if they could 'humiliate him in public'. Bailey writes, 'Presumably overnight they arrested a woman they claimed was "caught in the act of adultery" and held her for the showdown with Jesus.'[5]

Jesus responded very cleverly, effectively saying that the woman should not be stoned but doing so in such a way that he did not contradict the Law of Moses. Remember he lived in a society with no clear distinction between religious law and the law of the land.

But why was this a 'test'? It seems to me that his critics must have suspected that he would not support the stoning. In other words, he must have already had a reputation for not being entirely supportive of the law. This should be no surprise. According to Mark's Gospel, one of Jesus' first public acts was to break the law by picking grain on the Sabbath.[6] He was eventually arrested after an undoubtedly illegal protest in the Jerusalem Temple (see Chapters 16 and 17).[7]

Was this reputation about his attitude to law generally, to punishment, or to particular acts? It is fascinating to consider how he would have behaved if the 'criminal' had been a thief, murderer or a rapist. Sally asked why the Scribes and Pharisees wanted to punish only the woman, rather than the man with whom she was accused of committing adultery. This may be a crucial point.

'Adultery' had a specific meaning in the society of the time: it referred to a man having sex with someone else's wife. The marital status of the man was irrelevant to the charge. The book of Deuteronomy, part of the Torah (or Law of Moses) declares:

> *If a man is caught having sexual intercourse with another man's wife, both must be put to death: the man who has slept with her and the woman herself. You must banish this evil from Israel.*[8]

But this is *not* what is happening here! The Scribes and Pharisees do not appear to be following the Law of Moses themselves, as they have brought only the woman and not the man. This is a reminder that accusations of adultery often have a great deal to do with power. This was not particular to Jesus' society. It has been a feature of many cultures across time. As the theologian Walter Wink argues, it is a sign of an attitude that 'treats adultery as the ultimate sexual sin because it is the egregious violation of male property rights over women.'[9]

Christian feminists argue that Jesus was challenging an entire system, not only being compassionate in a one-off case.

'At the heart of the episode is precisely the redefining of sin,' says commentator Elizabeth Green. She argues that Jesus was challenging male assumptions about the sexual sinfulness of women.[10]

Prejudiced attitudes towards women continue in the interpretation of the passage. The story is nearly always headed, 'The woman caught in adultery', which keeps the focus on the woman's sin.[11]

But if Jesus had a problem with the adulterous man not being there alongside the woman, why did he not say so? Would his listeners have understood this point as implicit in his comments? Or would he have objected just as much to stoning both of them? Was he focusing on bigger issues than the letter of the law?

Like most female characters in the gospels, this woman's name is not mentioned. I find myself wondering if Jesus knew her, or knew of her, before this incident. We can only speculate. Did he regard her as more sinned against than sinning? Was he 'paternal' to her, as Heather suggested? Or 'judgemental', because he accepted the charge against her? Is the biblical scholar Jerome Neyrey correct when he says that Jesus was concerned with 'rescuing her from being a pawn' in his arguments with his opponents?[12]

It is not easy to guess Jesus' thoughts. This leaves us with one of the aspects of the story that drew the attention of our first-time readers. Why was Jesus writing on the ground?

There is a medieval tradition that Jesus was listing the sins of the accusers, although it is doubtful if he had time for this. Some suggest he was drawing attention away from the woman, who may have been naked. By looking down again after making his comment about casting stones, he allowed the embarrassed listeners to leave without having to look him in the eye. Another possibility is that he was taking control of the situation by undermining expectations. Commentator Gail O'Day suggests that Jesus was putting the Scribes and Pharisees on the same level as the woman by not talking to them.[13]

The Upside-down Bible

We don't necessarily have to choose between these explanations: there could well be more than one reason. Perhaps the simplest explanation is that Jesus was buying time as he thought about how to respond. Samantha found that the action made Jesus more 'human' for her. Even in mainstream Christian theology, Jesus is regarded as fully human. It's easy to forget that.

QUESTIONS

1. How would Jesus have behaved if he had been presented with both the man and the woman who had committed adultery? Would things have been any different?
2. What relevance does this story have for how we approach violence and crime today?
3. What conclusions do you draw about the personality and mood of Jesus?

NOTES

[1] Cited by Frederick Dale Bruner, *The Gospel of John: A Commentary* (William B. Eerdmans, 2012).
[2] Raymond E. Brown, *The Gospel According to John: I-XII* (Doubleday & Co., 1966).
[3] Matthew 5:21–22.
[4] Raymond E. Brown, *The Gospel According to John: I-XII* (Doubleday & Company, 1966).
[5] Kenneth E. Bailey, *Jesus through Middle Eastern Eyes: Cultural Studies in the Gospels* (SPCK, 2008).
[6] Mark 2:23–24.
[7] Mark 11:15–17.
[8] Deuteronomy 22:22.
[9] Walter Wink, *Engaging the Powers: Discernment and Resistance in a World of Domination* (Augsburg Fortress, 1992).
[10] Elizabeth E. Green, 'Making her case and reading it too: Feminist readings of the story of the woman taken in adultery' in *Ciphers in the Sand: Interpretations of the Woman Taken in Adultery (John 7:53– 811)*, ed. Larry J. Kreitzer and Deborah W. Rooke (Sheffield Academic Press, 2000).

11 Many thanks to Beth Howard for suggesting 'The men caught in hypocrisy' as an alternative title.

12 Jerome H. Neyrey, *The Gospel of John* (Cambridge University Press, 2007).

13 Gail R. O'Day, 'John' in *The Women's Bible Commentary*, ed.Carol A. Newsom and Sharon H. Ringe (Westminster John Knox Press, 1998).

15. Small rebellions

(Matthew 5:38–46)

This is a quote from Jesus. It forms part of a longer speech that can be found in Matthew's Gospel (Chapters 5–7). Parts of it also appear in Luke.

You have heard how it was said, 'Eye for eye and tooth for tooth.' But I say this to you: offer no resistance to the wicked. On the contrary, if anyone hits you on the right cheek, offer him the other as well; if someone wishes to go to law with you to get your tunic, let him have your cloak as well. And if anyone requires you to go one mile, go two miles with him.

Give to everyone who asks you, and if anyone wants to borrow, do not turn away.

You have heard how it was said, 'You will love your neighbour and hate your enemy.'

Language point

Translation: The translation of the phrase 'offer no resistance to the wicked' is controversial. Many argue that the Greek is referring specifically to violent resistance. Alternative translations include 'don't react violently to the one who is evil' and 'do not return evil for evil'.

Historical point

Under Roman law, soldiers could force civilians to carry their pack for a mile.

But I say this to you, love your enemies and pray for those who persecute you, so that you may be children of your Father in heaven, for he causes his sun rise on the bad as well as the good, and sends down rain to fall on the upright and the wicked alike. For if you love those who love you, what reward will you get? Do not even the tax collectors do as much?

REACTIONS

What are your feelings after reading this passage? Is Jesus' teaching here something that you want to follow? What do you think Jesus meant by 'offer no resistance to the wicked'?

INSIGHTS

This passage is responsible for two phrases that have entered into general vocabulary: 'Turn the other cheek' and 'Go the extra mile'. I went on social media in an attempt to find out what they mean to people today.

One of the first to respond declared, 'The former clearly has biblical connotations in my mind, while the latter none!' I found that several people associated the 'other cheek' phrase with Jesus but did not link the 'extra mile' with the Bible at all.

'"Going the extra mile" just makes me think of corporate management speak,' said one respondent. Another said '"Go the extra mile" has been appearing in my job applications.'

Not everyone was so negative about it. One person took it to mean, 'Being helpful and giving towards people even if you don't know them.' Another replied, 'My instinctive reaction is that it's easier said than done.'

More people were positive about turning the other cheek. One person offered the interpretation, 'Don't escalate a disagreement even if the other person is trying to.' Another described it as 'the ideal of pacifism'. He added, 'By offering your

The Upside-down Bible

other cheek for them to strike, you are showing that you have already forgiven them.' Someone else said that turning the other cheek was about 'clever ways of subverting social norms and standing up to authority'.

Others had major problems with the phrase. 'It feels like telling a person in a violent, oppressive situation to just put up with it,' said one respondent. 'This phrase can be used to dismiss complaints of mistreatment, invalidating the anger of the victim.' Someone else said that whatever the phrase's original meaning, it had been used 'to suggest there should be no challenge to abuses of power'.

The same mixture of attitudes was apparent when I showed people the whole passage.

'Taken literally, this is foolish advice,' said Jon. 'It allows anyone prepared to use violence to completely dominate those who follow this advice, and the lazy to live at the expense of others.' He felt that the phrase 'Give to everyone who asks of you' could encourage people to take even from those poorer than themselves.

That line came as a surprise to Adam, who said, 'The point about always giving to beggars is one I don't remember ever seeing before, despite going to chapel every day at school.'

Angie commented on the passage's implications for domestic violence. 'A woman who "turns the other cheek, gives her cloak and goes the second mile" could end up in a very dangerous situation very quickly,' she said. While Angie would not advocate responding with violence, she 'would think that walking away from the situation would be a good course of action'.

Despite this, Angie was quite keen on other aspects of the passage. She read it as saying, 'Consider the other person as another human being and respect that whilst abhorring their behaviour.' But she added, 'I imagine it's very hard to put this way of thinking into practice, however, if the persecution suffered has been real and devastating.'

Adam, who is a political activist, felt that while the passage could be used to promote passivity, it could also encourage nonviolent resistance. He suggested that carrying a Roman soldier's pack a second mile could be a way to get him punished and 'shaming someone by giving them all your clothes is a way to resist'.

Albert, an atheist pacifist, thought the passage was 'in danger of being interpreted too passively'. He explained, 'I want to resist "the wicked" as strongly as I can, but excluding armed tactics.'

REFLECTION

'Turn the other cheek', was a favourite passage with clergy who preached to slaves in eighteenth-century plantations. They said that God would reward the slaves if they accepted punishment without resistance or complaint. The passage is also quoted by people insisting that women must not object if their husbands are violent.

Given the use of this passage for such vile ends, I don't blame anyone for choosing to reject Jesus' words altogether. This passage has been of use to those who have an interest in keeping things the way they are, however unjust they may be.

At other times, the powerful have found the passage used against them — particularly when they want to wage war.

John 'Bert' Brocklesby was a 25-year-old Methodist lay preacher from South Yorkshire when The First World War broke out in 1914. There was outrage in his congregation when he preached against the war from the pulpit, quoting this passage. He found himself facing a tribunal when he was conscripted in 1916 and refused to fight. 'Would you turn the other cheek?' he was asked. 'That is our Christian duty, sir,' he replied. Sent to an army barracks, he again quoted biblical teaching. 'Do you not think those commands apply to individuals but not to states?' asked the commanding officer. 'They apply to both,' said Brocklesby.[1]

Shortly afterwards, Brocklesby was sentenced to death, although the sentence was commuted to ten years in prison.

This passage has posed a problem not only to those who want to resist injustice but to governments ordering people to go to war on their behalf. How do you teach people to reject all violence except when you order them to engage in it? Christianity became largely pro-war from the fourth century, after it became the official religion of the Roman Empire. Ever since, Christian rulers have struggled with dissidents who have rediscovered these teachings of Jesus for themselves, spoken out against warfare and refused to use violence. Jesus' words in this passage were favourites of the Anabaptist movement in the sixteenth century and the Quaker movement in the seventeenth, both of which rejected 'outward weapons' (to use a Quaker phrase).

The most common response to this position is that of the commanding officer just quoted: to suggest that the teachings apply to individuals in 'private' life but not when they are acting on behalf of states. The problem, as the theologian Stanley Hauerwas points out, is that 'This distinction between the private person and the bearer of an office is unknown to Jesus'.[2]

Other justifications for not following Jesus' teaching include the claim that it was meant only for priests. Yet the comment appears in Matthew's Gospel as part of a fairly lengthy speech said to have been given by Jesus from a hilltop to a general crowd (often referred to as 'the sermon on the mount'). In the sixteenth century, some taught that the teaching was a 'counsel of perfection', which we could never live up to, designed to make us realise our own sin.

There are others who say that if we are not persuaded by Jesus' teaching then there is more honesty in saying so, rather than claiming to believe in it while concluding that it does not apply to us.

I suggest that if we want to know what Jesus thought, we need to take this passage seriously. We have to ask if he really did intend people to ignore bullying and domestic abuse. To do this, we need to look at Jesus' background and his other

Small rebellions

words and actions and consider if this teaching has relevance to us today. Taking the passage seriously does not mean taking it simplistically.

Jesus begins by citing the Hebrew scriptures (which Christians call the Old Testament): 'Eye for eye and tooth for tooth'. This line is often quoted today in reference to vindictive punishments that are supposed to 'fit the crime'. But when it was developed, some centuries before Jesus' time, it would have sounded very different. Many cultures of the time operated on a far less controlled basis. If I killed you, then your family would attack my family in retaliation. My relatives would then kill more of your relatives, and so on. 'Eye for eye' prevented blood feuds and limited violence. This was a progressive policy in its context. Had certain right-wing newspapers been around at the time, they would probably have produced outraged editorials saying, 'Not massacring murderers' families! This is political correctness gone mad.'

Thus Jesus began by quoting a principle designed to limit violence and went beyond it. We need to remember the realities of power in Jesus' society. Palestine was occupied by the Romans. I have lost count of the number of sermons I have heard that say that Jesus had no problem with the Roman Empire. This usually goes along the lines of 'The people expected a political messiah, but Jesus was a spiritual messiah'. As we have seen, people at the time made no distinction between religion and politics (see Chapter 2 for more on this). However, scholars remain divided. Some still argue that Jesus had little interest in challenging political authorities as such. Others, such as Ched Myers, argue that Jesus was promoting *nonviolent* resistance to Rome.[3] Walter Wink suggests that Jesus wanted to resist the whole 'domination system' of unequal relationships, of which the Roman Empire was only a part. More recently, a few scholars such as Reza Aslan have argued that Jesus was really a supporter of violent revolution.[4]

Roman soldiers were allowed to force civilians to carry their packs for them. As you can imagine, this caused a lot of resentment amongst populations across the empire. The Roman authorities restricted the practice by banning soldiers from forcing a civilian to carry their pack further than a mile. There is limited evidence about how well this rule was enforced. There are, however, many accounts of Roman soldiers in various parts of the empire being punished for mistreating civilians. The authorities were clearly frightened that such abuses could trigger resentment or even rebellion.

How would you respond if ordered to carry a pack for a mile by a soldier of an occupying army? Undoubtedly the most common response would be to accept the order and the humiliation that comes with it. Alternatively, you could try to refuse, perhaps even attempting to fight the soldier. You were unlikely to have much success in using violence against the most powerful army in the world. Jesus suggests a third option: walk for another mile.

Some interpret this suggestion as an encouragement to show kindness to everyone, to love oppressors. It is argued that this fits in with Jesus' advice to love enemies and his friendship with tax collectors, sex workers and other outcasts

The 'kindness to oppressors' interpretation has been challenged by a number of writers, most famously Walter Wink.[5] We saw Adam's suggestion that going the second mile could be a way of getting the soldier into trouble. Wink asks us to imagine the soldier's surprise when a Jewish civilian offers to carry his pack further. As Wink puts it, 'The humour of this scene may have escaped us but it could scarcely have been lost on Jesus' hearers.' The soldier may be worried about being punished for violating the rules. The Jew has thus seized the initiative, taken back the power to make a choice and disturbed the balance of power.

Wink may be overstating his case. Not all soldiers would fear punishment in this situation; some might take advantage of it. I can imagine others would just think the civilian was being weird, snatch the pack back and barely think of the matter again.

But Wink surely has a point: at least some soldiers would be thrown off balance by it, and for some there would be concern about punishment. The activist and Anglican priest Keith Hebden says that going the second mile is 'about using the rules of the oppressor to your own creative advantage when you have little left to fight with'.[6]

Jesus was talking to people who were used to being abused. Jewish civilians ruled by Roman soldiers, women beaten by their husbands, slaves and employees exploited by their bosses. How should they react when hit on the right cheek? Turn the left. Is this a phrase that would be chosen by someone encouraging them to accept abuse?

What does an abusive husband or domineering boss expect when he uses violence? Surely the most common response of a frightened person is to cower, to tremble, to back away. This is the response that some who enjoy exercising violent power over others are looking for. In contrast, turning the other cheek sounds like a very odd thing to do. The phrase might sound normal to us, but that is only because it has entered the language as a clichéd phrase since Jesus' time.

To slap someone on the right cheek (with the right hand) requires a backhanded blow. C. F Andrews, an English comrade of Gandhi's, was one of several scholars to point out the significance of this in Jesus' time.[7] A backhanded blow was how supposed inferiors were disciplined: husbands backhanded their wives, soldiers backhanded civilians, bosses backhanded their slaves. It was considered far more insulting than being hit directly in the face.

When I first read this explanation, it sounded as if it involved a bit of guesswork about attitudes at the time. Then I came across a fact which changed my mind: if a Roman citizen backhanded another Roman citizen, the fine imposed as punishment was *a hundred times higher* than if he had simply hit him with his fist. That's how insulting it was.[8]

Andrews argued that Jesus was not encouraging submission but a sort of nonviolent defiance. You hit me. I will not cower, and fighting back would be useless. But I will not be intimidated. I will calmly stand my ground and simply turn my other cheek. It would require considerable self-possession, not to say courage, to do this. Some go as far as to argue that Jesus was encouraging people to demand that their abusers punched them directly, thereby treating them as equals.

You can probably see how the third instruction can be interpreted in a similar way. If someone sues you so heavily that you are reduced to giving your own coat away, go so far as to give away the rest of your clothes. The Torah, or Jewish law, forbids the taking of a coat from someone who was being sued, as no one should be reduced to such extreme poverty.[9] Jesus' words suggest that this law was not being enforced in practice. By taking off all your clothes, you made a symbolic statement about the effect of your opponent's legal action against you. In the culture of the time, nakedness was shaming not only for the person with no clothes on but for those who saw them while naked. You would thus shame those who saw you – such as your opponent or the judge.

Walter Wink argues that Jesus' teaching in this passage is an illustration of Jesus' 'third way' – a rejection of both passivity and violence. Wink, like Gandhi and many other nonviolent activists, is keen to emphasise that active nonviolence is not a halfway position between submission and violence, but is more radical than both.

It seems that references to turning cheeks and walking extra miles are examples relevant to Jesus' own time. Keith Hebden writes, 'None of these are straightforward commands, but rather a blueprint for a new way of thinking.'[10] So how can we apply the principles behind Jesus' words to our own context?

One example that occurs to me involves John Wesley, the founder of Methodism. It is said that one day Wesley encountered on a narrow pathway a man who was not a fan of Methodism. He expected Wesley to make way for him. The passive response would be to step out of the way and let him pass. The aggressive way would be to refuse and push past him.

Wesley chose the third way. The man shouted, 'I never make way for a fool! Wesley stepped aside, saying, 'I always do!'[11]

Sometimes when I have quoted these examples, I have been accused of encouraging people to be 'rude' or 'bitchy'. This is a reminder that judging the right response in the context can be a challenge. Wink writes, 'One could easily misuse Jesus' advice vindictively; that is why it must not be separated from the command to love enemies.'[12]

The call to love enemies causes confusion and varied reactions. I sometimes joke that I need to have enemies in order to fulfil Jesus' instruction to love them. Hauerwas puts it more seriously when he says that 'a people of truth is sure to have enemies'.[13] Living by Jesus' teaching will attract hostility from those committed to dominant values and particularly from people who benefit from the status quo. If we follow Jesus' teaching to love them, then perhaps we can – to use Angie's phrase – consider the other person as human.

The interpretations of Wink and Andrews are not, of course, the only way of reading this passage, or even the only way of doing so that rejects submission to injustice. Stanley Hauerwas writes that 'Nonretaliation is not a strategy to get what we want by other means'. Hauerwas suggests that the teaching is meant for a voluntary community of Jesus' followers – whether the community that travelled around Palestine with Jesus, or a voluntary community today. He argues that Jesus' teaching is 'not addressed to individuals but to the community that Jesus begins ... You cannot live by the demands of the sermon on your own, but that is the point. The demands of the sermon are designed to make us depend on God and one another.'[14]

Hauerwas' view is similar to that of the German theologian and activist Dietrich Bonhoeffer. He said he could not follow Jesus' teachings without being part of a community founded on faith in Jesus' resurrection. Living in this way is a 'visible act' which separates the community of Jesus' followers from the world.[15] Bonhoeffer's own visible acts against injustice led to his execution by the Nazi regime in 1945. He was 39.

Where does all this leave Jesus' advice to offer 'no resistance to the wicked'? The translation of the word rendered as 'resistance' is controversial. Most uses of it imply violence. One Bible translation, the Scholars' Version, renders the line, 'Don't react violently against the one who is evil.'[16] John Henson's looser translation declares, 'It's time to put a stop to the game of paying back wrongs.'[17]

If we look at the rest of Jesus' life, we find many instances of him challenging evil, and on one occasion doing so physically (if not necessarily violently), as we will see in the next chapter. Even without getting into debates about translation, it seems reasonable to assume on the basis of Jesus' life that what he was rejecting was either violent resistance or the practice of viewing others with an attitude of hatred.

There are other parts of this passage that are quoted less often. As Adam noticed, the injunction to give to everyone who begs from you was not mentioned in the chapel of his private school. Some suggest that Jesus was talking only about how members of the community should behave towards each other. This seems conveniently limiting.

Rarely has a passage of the Bible been used so often both to excuse abuse and to encourage resistance. Jesus spoke about the rules and practices of his society and suggested some pretty unusual responses to them. How do we respond to the laws and conventions of our own society, particularly those we consider unfair? As Wink puts it, 'The rules are Caesar's, but how one responds to the rules is God's, and Caesar has no power over that.'[18]

Not all of the situations covered by Jesus' comments involve large-scale political conflicts. They are certainly all political, but some of them are more about how political injustice is manifested in everyday life. If we want to adapt Jesus' examples to our own lives, we need to think on an everyday level. I am reminded of the lyrics of a song by the Christian band Jars of Clay: 'Give us days that are filled with small rebellions – senseless, brutal acts of kindness from our souls.'

QUESTIONS

1. What might loving enemies involve in practice?
2. What do you make of the idea that Jesus was promoting active nonviolence?
3. What, in your own life and the society you live in, might be the equivalents of turning the other cheek, walking a second mile or removing your clothes?

NOTES

[1] John 'Bert' Brocklesby, *Escape from Paganism* (Unpublished memoirs, stored at Friends House Library, London).

[2] Stanley Hauerwas, *Matthew* (SCM Press, 2006).

[3] Ched Myers, *Binding the Strong Man: A Political Reading of Mark's story of Jesus* (Orbis, Books 1988).

[4] Reza Aslan, *Zealot: The Life and Times of Jesus of Nazareth* (Westbourne Press, 2014).

[5] Walter Wink, *Engaging the Powers: Discernment and Resistance in a World of Domination* (Augsburg Fortress, 1992).

[6] Keith Hebden, *Seeking Justice: The Radical Compassion of Jesus* (Circle Books, 2012).

[7] Terrence J. Rynne, *Gandhi and Jesus: The Saving Power of Nonviolence* (Orbis Books, 2008).

[8] Walter Wink, *Jesus and Nonviolence: A Third Way* (Fortress Press, 2003).

[9] Deuteronomy 24:12–13.

[10] Hebden, *Seeking Justice*.

[11] There appear to be several versions of this story but the essence of them is the same.

[12] Wink, *Engaging the Powers*.

[13] Hauerwas, *Matthew*.

[14] Hauerwas, *Matthew*.

[15] Dietrich Bonhoeffer, *Discipleship*, trans. Barbara Green and Reinhard Krauss (Fortress, 2001).

[16] Robert Funk et al., *The Five Gospels: What Did Jesus Really Say?* (HarperOne, 1997).

[17] John Henson, *Good as New: A Radical Retelling of the Scriptures* (O Books, 2004).

[18] Wink, *Engaging the Powers*.

16. Jesus takes direct action

(Mark 11:11–18)

This incident is described, with different wording, in all four gospels. This is from Mark's Gospel, probably the earliest surviving written account.

Jesus entered Jerusalem and went into the temple; and when he had surveyed it all, as it was late by now, he went out to Bethany with the Twelve.

Next day ... they reached Jerusalem and he went into the Temple and began driving out the men selling and buying there; he upset the tables of the money changers and the seats of the dove sellers. Nor would he allow anyone to carry anything through the Temple.

Language point
Money-changers: Businesspeople who exchanged currencies into the currency used to pay the Temple tax.

Dove-sellers: Doves were the cheapest acceptable sacrifice in the Temple; the doves were being sold for this purpose.

Historical point
The Jerusalem Temple was the centre of Jewish worship. At this point, the Romans occupying Palestine allowed Jewish worship to continue in the Temple within certain limits. The Temple authorities encouraged loyalty to the Roman Empire.

And he taught them and said, 'Does not scripture say: "My house shall be called a house of prayer for all peoples?" But you have made it into a bandits' den'

This came to the ears of the chief priests and the scribes, and they tried to find some way of doing away with him; they were afraid of him because the people were carried away by his teaching.

And when evening came, he went out of the city.

REACTIONS

Take a moment to consider your feelings after reading this passage. Do you feel encouraged? Worried? Uncomfortable? Inspired? How do you feel about Jesus' behaviour? Do you consider it to be violent?

INSIGHTS

'I've been to the Wailing Wall and seen how much it matters to people,' said Beccy, who is Jewish. The Wailing Wall is the only part of the Jerusalem Temple that remains standing. The rest was destroyed by Roman forces as they suppressed a Jewish rebellion about forty years after the time of Jesus.

Beccy said that her experience of Jerusalem helps her to understand 'how shocking what Jesus did would have been'. She added, 'But it occurs to me it also adds another layer: how upsetting it might have been to Jesus to see the Temple being used in a way he didn't think was right.'

The passage came as a shock to some who were unfamiliar with it. 'Definitely the part about him turning over tables and seats was surprising for me,' said Claire. 'I was strongly under the impression that Jesus was a peaceful person and those sorts of actions don't fit in with that.'

Jesus' action in the Temple continues to divide opinion. Paula said, 'Jesus is very intolerant of people who aren't religious.' She

The Upside-down Bible

added, 'You could almost feel him in the modern day being like ISIS, coming in and purifying religion.'

In contrast, Sarah said, 'I love this passage.' She explained, 'To me this is valuable because it is about actions – and direct action – and also about the right to rebel against religious leaders who are greedy.'

What motivated Jesus? 'Anger that a place of worship was being used to make money,' said Jon, who remembers the story from primary school. 'Anger and hatred,' said Angie. Claire suggested that Jesus felt 'like he is carrying out the will of God'.

Kyon thought that Jesus was tackling 'a spiritless society only governed by laws but without understanding compassion or a spiritual aspect'. Adam said, 'Jesus is challenging capitalism, and in modern terms, the commercialisation of space.'

Is it fair to describe Jesus' behaviour as 'violent'?

Paula said, 'Yes, he is violent.' She added, 'He's coming in with twelve people, overturning the tables, being aggressive.'

Sarah said, 'It isn't violent against people – he doesn't attack people, he turns over tables and chairs and stops people from doing business but he doesn't attack anyone – that's an important distinction.'

Claire disapproved of Jesus' behaviour but did not consider it to be violent. She said that no one has 'a right to be intimidating'. But she thought Jesus' actions should not be classified as violent because they were against 'objects, not people'.

In complete contrast, Alice thought Jesus was violent but still approved of his actions. 'I think that whether something is violent or not is different to whether something is moral or not,' she explained. 'Jesus' violence was addressing a bigger wrong and didn't do more harm than it had to do.' She said she would take a different view if Jesus had, for example, started stabbing the money-changers.

Angie said, 'The sense I get is that his anger overtook his better judgement.' But Sarah defended him: 'I'm very much in favour of action rather than inaction in the face of something which is wrong.'

What did Jesus achieve? Kyon, who is a Shia Muslim, said, 'It seems to me that Jesus was not only turning the tables upside-down but in fact he was turning the whole society upside-down.' Alice, who is a Jewish anarchist, suggested that Jesus had 'a long-term strategy' of which this protest was only part.

Beccy wondered whether Jesus wanted to be 'faithful or successful'. She explained, 'If Jesus' aim is to live to a ripe old age, he's being a bit foolish.' She thought the other possibility is that Jesus wanted to 'make as much of an impression as possible in a much more limited space of time'.

Beccy also questioned how Jesus had managed single-handedly to stop anyone carrying anything through the Temple. Was it by force or could it be due to his commanding personality? At first glance, she said, the protest seems impulsive and instinctive, but she noted that Jesus had looked round the Temple the day beforehand, as if he were planning the protest. 'Once you take that into account, it's clear that he's really thought it through,' she concluded.

Alice thought that Jesus' behaviour was in contrast to his comments about turning the other cheek (see Chapter 15). She said, 'I guess the question for people is: For whom do you turn the other cheek and for whom do you turn the tables?'

REFLECTION

When I was at primary school, the local vicar would come in every Wednesday and tell us stories about Jesus. He said that Jesus showed us the right way of doing things. Looking back, I doubt that he expected us to copy Jesus' behaviour by overturning tables.

The impression I gained at school was that Jesus was surprised to find commercial activity going on in the Temple. There are many descriptions that could be applied to Jesus in this passage. The readers quoted above described him variously as 'aggressive', 'angry' and 'courageous'. But there is one thing that Jesus definitely wasn't: surprised. Economic activity was a normal part of the Temple's function. The Temple was not just a religious centre but a political and economic one.

The Roman occupiers tolerated the Temple's existence as long as the High Priest and his colleagues encouraged loyalty to the Roman Empire. Prayers for the emperor were offered in the Temple every day. The annual Temple tax was paid in a currency not used in everyday life so in the run-up to Passover every year, money-changers set up stalls in the Temple forecourt. If visitors to the Temple wanted to make sacrifices to seek forgiveness for sins, they could buy the animals on offer. Doves – or, as we would probably call them, pigeons – were the cheapest acceptable sacrifice.

Some Jews supported this system, others did not. Historians differ when asked about the extent of opposition to the Temple authorities. It is clear that the Temple's leaders were often accused of being corrupt and resented for their loyalty to the Roman Empire. Jesus was far from being the only Jew to have a problem with the Temple's leadership and the way it was run. The Temple was a political power centre, the seat of the client rulers who kept the Jewish population subservient to Rome.

Alternatives to the Temple were developing. The Pharisees, while accepting the Temple in principle, emphasised the need to follow Jewish law more in the home and in everyday life. Members of another group, the Essenes, went further. They withdraw into the desert to set up their own community, denouncing the Temple and its 'false' priests.

In the midst of this political and religious turmoil, Jesus and his followers arrived in Jerusalem. They turned up shortly before Passover, the leading Jewish festival, which celebrates the liberation of the Israelites centuries earlier. Talk of freedom was in the air. According to Josephus, a Jewish historian who lived in the first century, Roman troops were often stationed near the Temple at Passover time, as the authorities were particularly nervous of rebellion.

Above, we saw Jon, like many readers of this passage,

suggesting that Jesus was angry about a religious building being used for commerce. It's an understandable assumption. You may have heard the same claim made in sermons. If we look at the historical background, it quickly becomes clear that there is a problem with it. Commerce was an everyday part of the Temple's activity. It allowed people to buy animals for sacrifices. A protest against trade at the Temple would be a protest against the very nature of the Temple itself, rather than an objection to a recent development.

The traders, disciples and passers-by would have recognised that at several points Jesus was using words from the Hebrew scriptures (which Christians call the Old Testament). When Jesus spoke of a 'bandits' den', he was quoting the prophet Jeremiah. Centuries earlier, Jeremiah had used the word 'bandits' to describe those in charge at the Temple. He said that they 'exploit the stranger, the orphan and the widow' and 'shed innocent blood' but expect to be safe from God's anger because they worship in the Temple. He said the Temple would be destroyed if they continued to behave in this way.[1]

Biblical scholar Morna Hooker believes that Jesus was following in the tradition of Jeremiah, seeing the sacrifices in the Temple as invalid because they were offered by corrupt priests. According to Hooker, it is the priests, not the money-changers and pigeon-sellers, who are the bandits. She suggests that Jesus saw much of the worship offered in the Temple as a sham – hence he sought to prevent sacrifices by throwing out those buying and selling.[2]

· Others say that this does not really explain the focus on the money-changers and pigeon-sellers. They believe that Jesus was protesting against economic exploitation. Is this taking us back to the idea that he was objecting to commerce in a religious building? Not necessarily. He may have opposed the excessive rates charged by the traders and money-changers. There seem to have been various attempts at the time to keep the prices down. A few decades after Jesus' time, a rabbi called Simeon successfully campaigned to reduce the price of sacrificial pigeons.[3]

The Upside-down Bible

What if Jesus was objecting not just to prices but to the whole system? The money-changers were there because of a Temple tax imposed on people already heavily burdened by Roman taxes. The pigeons were sold to the poorest worshippers. Some believe that Jesus was outraged that such people were pressurised to spend their limited money before they could engage in worship. Biblical scholar Ched Myers argues that Jesus was not merely a 'reformist' concerned with lower prices. Myers writes, 'It is the ruling-class interests in control of the commercial practices in the Temple market that Jesus is attacking.'[4]

Myers believes that Jesus was not opposing only the Jewish establishment but the Roman authorities behind it. Keith Hebden argues that 'Jesus saw something in the Temple that his companions had not yet understood ... It was nothing more than the empire's agent. Its presence was dependent entirely on Roman largesse and peasant blood, sweat, and tears.'[5] To Hebden, Jesus was resisting all forms of oppression, standing not just against one temple or empire but against the world's 'domination system'.

Is this convincing? Your answer may depend on what view you have formed of Jesus from his other words and actions. The notion that Jesus was trying to change the system is encouraged by an additional detail that appears in Matthew's Gospel. According to Matthew, blind and disabled people, along with children, came into the Temple during Jesus' protest.[6] None of these groups were usually allowed in the Temple and were excluded from making sacrifices. Jesus and his disciples appear to have broken this rule and invited them in.[7]

We can also approach this passage from another angle: why did Jesus choose *this* form of protest. Claire thought it did not seem consistent with the impression we usually have of Jesus. Previously he had relied on words. Now he puts his hands to use to overturn tables and scatter coins.

Beccy noticed that, according to Mark's Gospel, Jesus had looked round the Temple the evening before and left when it was late. This suggests a reconnaissance to plan the action for the following day. The idea that Jesus would not allow anyone to carry anything through the Temple would be bizarre if he acted alone while his disciples watched. The Temple was far too big for that. If his followers joined in – lots of them, not just the 'Twelve' – they may have blockaded the entrances. If we consider these points, Jesus' action looks less like a spontaneous outburst of anger and appears instead as a well-planned protest.

Was this an attempt at revolution? Did Jesus expect that he and his followers would keep control of the Temple and inspire an uprising? If so, he must have been optimistic to say the least. A small group of unarmed people were unlikely to hold off the Temple authorities, let alone the Roman troops that could be sent to back them up. It seems that Jesus and his comrades left the Temple that evening, having maintained their protest for less than a day. The traders would have gathered up their scattered coins, the entrances opened again and the Temple's business gone back to normal.

Jesus may not have even managed this much. Some historians doubt that the protest could have happened on the scale described in the gospels. Biblical scholar Eduard Schweizer insists, 'It would have been almost impossible for Jesus to have cleared the vast Temple court – especially to have done so without causing the intervention of the Jewish Temple police or of the Roman military stationed nearby.' He suggests that, 'It is more likely that Jesus, in a symbolic way, cleared only a limited area of the Temple court.'[8]

Whether it was the whole Temple or only part of it, the purpose of the protest seems to have been as much about symbolism as anything else. I am reminded of protests in our own society against nuclear weapons, the arms trade or fossil fuels. People who block an arms factory may disrupt its activities for a few hours or a few days. They may well feel that delaying its work is worthwhile in itself, even for such a short period. This, however, is not usually the only reason for such protests. They often have a symbolic value and can gain publicity for the cause.

Think of Gandhi. As a leader of the nonviolent movement for Indian independence, Mohandas Gandhi made repeated and effective use of symbolic, headline-grabbing actions. Criticising the British Empire's monopoly on salt production, he led a peaceful march to the sea. In full view of international television cameras, he scooped up salt from the water and encouraged people to begin manufacturing and selling salt without permission from the authorities. This was unlikely to have made much financial impact on India's British rulers, but its symbolic value was enormous. The cameras that filmed the Salt March were not incidental to it. Gandhi knew very well how important it was to ensure that they were there.

It is not only the shallow and egotistical who are concerned with publicity! It is also very relevant to those seeking to promote a cause that they believe in.

Was this what Jesus was up to? Was Beccy right to suggest that Jesus was aiming to make a big impression in a short time? The historian Anthony Le Donne argues that Jesus was relatively unknown when he arrived in the city. He may have been 'the popular faith healer and teacher from the north' but in Jerusalem he was just another pilgrim. Le Donne suggests that at this point Jesus realised 'he would have to do something dramatic to get his movement noticed'.[9]

If Le Donne is right, then Jesus succeeded. According to the gospels, it was after the Temple protest that the authorities came together to work out how to get rid of him. Many within the Temple leadership may have genuinely believed that they were keeping the people safe by preventing rebellion against Rome – and retaliation *from* Rome. Jesus may have thought them naïve: Rome was not going to allow its concessions to Jewish autonomy to continue forever.

Here is one of the great questions for students of Jesus: how did Jesus come to be seen as such a threat to the Roman Empire and their puppet rulers? We cannot know, although it seems likely that the Temple protest had something to do with it. Within days of this action, Jesus had been arrested and condemned to death.

Was Jesus violent? The readers quoted above had a wide range of views. At one end of the spectrum, Paula compared Jesus to ISIS. At the other, Sarah saw Jesus' action as nonviolent.

Pictures of Jesus' protest in the Temple often show him using a whip. The whip is mentioned only in John's Gospel, where the wording seems to suggest that he used it to drive out sheep and cattle that were on sale.[10] The other three gospels make no mention of physical violence in the protest.

Jesus may certainly have seemed aggressive, which some, such as Paula, regard as a type of violence. Others, such as Sarah and Claire, say that violence is about physical harm. Furthermore we do not know anything about Jesus' demeanour as he carried out this protest. We do not know if he was red-faced and shouting, or if he calmly explained his reasons to the traders before pushing over their tables.

The theologian Stanley Hauerwas writes, 'At the very least, those who would use Jesus' actions against the money-changers to justify war need to acknowledge that Jesus did not kill the money-changers.'[11]

Whether violent or not, Jesus' actions were in protest *against* the violence of the Roman Empire and the Temple elite. The violence of protesters tends to attract more attention than the routine violence of unjust systems.

Nowadays, the phrase 'direct action' is sometimes used as a synonym for unlawful protest. This is a rather sloppy use of the term. It refers to an action, whether legal or not, that involves preventing injustice directly, rather than asking someone else to do so for you. If you oppose the sale of weapons to dictators, you might write to the government about it. If the government continues regardless, you might decide to impede the sale of such weapons by disrupting an arms fair. Both of these are forms of activism. The latter is also direct action, because you would be trying to stop something directly, rather than calling on the authorities to do so.

In the light of Jesus' Temple protest, I find it difficult to see how anyone can argue that followers of Jesus should never consider taking direct action. I suspect this was not the lesson that the vicar who visited my primary school had in mind.

QUESTIONS

1. What do you think motivated Jesus' action?
2. In what ways was Jesus successful and unsuccessful?
3. How can we learn from Jesus' action today?

NOTES

[1] Jeremiah 7:1–11.
[2] Morna D. Hooker, *The Gospel According to St Mark* (A & C Black, 1991).
[3] Cited by Joachim Jeremias, *Jerusalem in the Time of Jesus: An Investigation into Economic and Social Conditions during the New Testament Period* (Fortress, 1969).
[4] Ched Myers, *Binding the Strong Man: A Political Reading of Mark's Story of Jesus* (Orbis Books, 1988).
[5] Keith Hebden, *Seeking Justice: The Radical Compassion of Jesus* (Circle Books, 2012).
[6] Matthew 21:14–15.
[7] Stanley Hauerwas, *Matthew* (SCM Press, 2006).
[8] Eduard Schweizer, *The Good News According to Mark* (John Knox Press, 1970).
[9] Anthony Le Donne, *Historical Jesus: What Can We Know and How Can We Know It?* (William B. Eerdmans, 2011).
[10] John 2:13–17.
[11] Hauerwas, *Matthew*.

17. Jesus makes a choice

(Matthew 26:47–57)

This is an account of Jesus' comments as he was arrested. The incident is described, with variations, in all four gospels. This is from Matthew. The passage begins as Jesus is talking with his followers in the Garden of Gethsemane in Jerusalem. He is approached by Judas, who has accepted money to betray him.

Suddenly while Jesus was still speaking, Judas, one of the Twelve, appeared, and with him a large number of men armed with swords and clubs, sent by the chief priests and elders of the people.

Now the traitor had arranged a sign with them, saying, 'The one I kiss, he is the man. Arrest him.'

So he went up to Jesus at once and said, 'Greetings, Rabbi,' and kissed him.

Jesus said to him, 'My friend, do what you are here for.'

Then they came forward, seized Jesus and arrested him.

The Upside-down Bible

And suddenly, one of the followers of Jesus grasped his sword and drew it; he struck the high priest's servant and cut off his ear.

Jesus then said, 'Put your sword back, for all who draw the sword will die by the sword.

'Or do you think that I cannot appeal to my Father, who would promptly send more than twelve legions of angels to my defence? But then, how would the scriptures be fulfilled that say this is the way it must be?'

It was at this time that Jesus said to the crowds, 'Am I a bandit, that you had to set out to capture me with swords and clubs? I sat teaching in the Temple day after day and you never laid a hand on me. Now all this has happened to fulfil the prophecies in scripture.'

Then all the disciples deserted him and ran away.

The men who had arrested Jesus led him off to the house of Caiaphas the high priest, where the scribes and the elders were assembled.

REACTIONS

Take a moment to think about how you feel after reading this passage. Can you imagine yourself in the scenario described? Which of Jesus' words appeal to you or put you off?

INSIGHTS

'Jesus is impressively calm,' said Adam. 'But also, in a strange way, annoyingly calm.'

Angie suggested that Jesus was 'not frightened and very calm' because he was expecting his arrest and felt he had the backing of his father.

Beccy said, 'Jesus' power comes from his vulnerability.' She found Jesus' attitude to be 'beautiful' amidst the drama of the story: 'These armed men massed against him and Judas betraying him in such a dramatic way and the way Jesus demonstrates he's more powerful is actively not through the sword, it's through not retaliating.'

Why did he encourage his followers not to use the sword? 'Probably he saw that his supporters were outnumbered and would have been killed if they had resisted,' said Jon. 'By giving himself up his disciples were able to escape. So the comments about the sword may have just been practical advice for that particular situation.'

In contrast, Albert said, 'I have a straightforward pacifist approach – responding without force of arms is the appropriate way to behave.' That did not make him impressed with Jesus' approach. He explained, 'I would expect a proper nonviolent revolutionary to have a more sophisticated approach than meek self-sacrifice. I'd go for something a bit more activist-Gandhian.'

Beccy, however, thought that Jesus' decision was about 'nonviolent resistance'. Adam said that Jesus was right to reject the sword, as he was discouraging his disciples from dying for him when he was prepared to die himself.

Angie sympathised with Jesus' view that those who take up the sword will die by the sword. She added, 'In my opinion if everyone lived by this message the world would be a better place, but unfortunately this is not the case.'

She also commented on the violence of Jesus' opponents: 'It seems like Jesus is saying that because he has never been violent in the past, their use of violence to capture him is wholly unnecessary.' Beccy suggested that by reminding his listeners of when he had taught in the Temple, Jesus was contrasting the image of a teacher with that of a warrior.

Some readers were put off by Jesus' comments about prophecy and scripture. Angie felt that Jesus seemed to be saying that the future is pre-ordained. She said, 'I struggle with this concept because although I agree that he was right to tell his followers to not fight back with swords, I'm not sure I agree with the concept that an unpleasant fate or situation cannot be avoided via other means.' Albert was more blunt, saying, 'I don't think that being fatalistic about a situation is the way to change the world or even to inspire people.'

But Beccy, who is from a Jewish background, doubted that Jesus had really said the words about prophecy and legions of angels. She explained, 'It seems as if it's written to show that Jesus fulfilled messianic expectations – he had the power but chose not to use it.' She said that Jesus' followers might have felt that their movement had been defeated when he was arrested.

Angie was the only one to mention the people carrying out the arrest. She interpreted the passage as meaning that 'Judas and these men were the messengers sent by others, and Jesus was God's messenger, and in some ways they all seem like they are following orders from someone else'.

Do Jesus' words still have relevance today? 'I don't see anything particularly useful here in general terms,' said Jon, 'in terms of when violence should or shouldn't be used.'

Adam gave a much shorter answer to the question: 'Lots of relevance. Jesus is calling for pacifism.'

REFLECTION

It's one of the most dramatic stories in the gospels. To have been part of it must have been confusing, noisy, terrifying. Written accounts can show only one person speaking at a time but they were surely speaking over the top of each other. There was the noise of the men grabbing Jesus, someone lashing out with a sword, Jesus' calm and firm words, the mixed shouts and comments of the disciples. It would have been difficult to hear anything clearly.

All four gospels give a fairly similar account of Jesus' arrest, with varied details. In all of them, he seems surprisingly calm and controlled. This was one of the main points noticed by the readers quoted above. I wonder if their response would have been different if I had shown them a slightly longer passage, which included Jesus' behaviour before this incident. Jesus had just shared the Passover meal with his disciples – his last meal before his death. They then went to the Garden of Gethsemane. According to Mark:

> *He began to feel terror and anguish. And he said to them, 'My soul is sorrowful to the point of death. Wait here, and stay awake.' And going on a little further he threw himself on the ground and prayed that, if it were possible, this hour might pass him by. 'Abba, Father!' he said. 'For you everything is possible. Take this cup away from me. But let it be as you, not I would have it.' He came back and found them sleeping.*[1]

In this passage, the teacher and activist suddenly appears simply as a frightened human being. Each gospel writer adds his own details. Luke says that 'his sweat fell to the ground like great drops of blood'.[2] If we believe the gospels' accounts, then Jesus' prayer clearly had an effect on him, for he was a model of calmness by the time he was arrested.

Some readers are troubled by Jesus' comments about prophecy. As Angie and Albert both noted, it sounds rather fatalistic. Jesus seems to be saying that his arrest and death cannot be avoided, but this does not mean that every aspect of the future is set in stone. Admittedly this is still troubling for some people.

Many scholars share Beccy's doubts about whether Jesus really did say these words. Some suggest they are 'editorial commentary' added by Matthew.[3] It's possible that Jesus' followers may have taken his arrest and execution as a sign that their movement had failed. Even after experiencing Jesus' resurrection, some probably still wondered why he had not triumphed over his opponents in a more obvious way. The words here could be taken as an explanation. As the New Testament scholar Morna Hooker puts it, 'Jesus knows precisely what is going to happen and is in control of the situation.'[4]

The gospel writers are telling us that it was not the people with weapons who were on top of events, but the man who refused to fight.

In contrast, the people arresting him are made to look rather silly. They have turned up heavily armed to tackle a small group of people, some of whom can barely stay awake. Ched Myers, biblical scholar and peace activist, writes that the scene 'reeks of the overkill so typical of covert state action against civilian dissidents'.[5]

How should we take Jesus' comments about his ability to call on angels to help him if he wished to do so? Again, this could be a later edition to the story to reassure those troubled by Jesus' apparent lack of power. It could also be taken as an assertion of a different type of power.

Throughout the last two thousand years, there have been Christians who have made a contrast between two types of power. Admittedly, these have not always been the most prominent and influential Christians. It has tended to be those with anti-authority tendencies who contrast the power of God with the powers of violence and money. Alfred Salter was a British Quaker activist and politician. Campaigning against the First World War in 1914, he urged everyone to make a choice: the religion of material power or the religion of spiritual power. To put it in more modern language, we might talk about the power of love and justice against the power of guns and tanks.

So Jesus' statement about angels may have been a comment about where power really lies. This fits in with some of his other comments here. Jesus managed to be ironic even while he was being arrested. He pointed out that they could have arrested him when he taught in the Temple. He knew very well why they did not: they waited until they had the cover of darkness and no audience.

Jesus said that they were treating him like a bandit – or, as we might put it, like a terrorist. In the eyes of the authorities, Jesus probably *was* a terrorist: he threatened the existing order and the careful power relations between Jerusalem and Rome, whether or not he used violence to do so.

Jesus makes a choice

What about the violence in this passage – the sword attack and Jesus' response? The story of Jesus' arrest seems to have been a tale that grew in the telling. In Mark, the earliest gospel, someone with Jesus draws his sword and cuts off the ear of the High Priest's servant. In Matthew (slightly later), Jesus has more words to say at this point. Luke goes further, telling us that Jesus not only rebuked the person who had drawn the sword but healed the servant's ear. By the time we get to John, the last of the biblical gospels to be written, the servant has been given a name and it is said to have been Jesus' friend Simon Peter who struck him with his sword.

The accumulation of details need not worry us, even if many of them are not factually accurate. Behind this tradition there was clearly an awareness that one of the people carrying out the arrest had been struck with a sword by someone with Jesus. But Jesus refused to use violence to defend himself – or to let someone else use violence for him.

Was Jesus' rejection of the sword a one-off decision or a ruling for evermore? We saw Jon's view that it was a practical decision in the circumstances: Jesus and his followers were outnumbered. Jesus, however, seems to have said more than this. 'All who draw the sword will die by the sword.' It is at the very least a description of the reality that violence begets more violence. Arguably, it is an encouragement never to resort to weapons.

Tertullian, a North African theologian in the late second and early third century, said that in saying these words Jesus had 'disarmed every soldier'. This was before the Roman Empire domesticated Christianity by making it the official religion of the empire in the fourth century, after which Christian leaders were cheerfully blessing armies.

There are a few objections to Tertullian's view. Some say that if Jesus' followers were carrying swords it must have been acceptable to use them. This argument is rather threadbare: we are not even told that the person concerned was a close follower of Jesus.

The Upside-down Bible

There is a stronger objection: many say that we should not make a commitment to pacifism – or any other position – solely on the basis of one comment from Jesus without looking at the rest of his teaching. The pacifist theologian Stanley Hauerwas himself warns against making a case for pacifism in this way. He argues, 'Arguments for Christian nonviolence, just as arguments for the Christian justification of violence, depend on how the story is told and the kind of community that exists to tell the story.'[6] For Hauerwas, it is only possible to follow Jesus in a voluntary community of committed disciples. In such a community, people support each other in a commitment to the nonviolent way demonstrated by Jesus.

Opponents of pacifism are understandably keen to quote other comments by Jesus that seem to support the use of violence. Reza Aslan is a historian who argues that Jesus supported violent rebellion. He points to a passage in Luke's Gospel in which Jesus talks to his disciples:

> He said to them, 'When I sent you out without purse or haversack or sandals, were you short of anything?' 'No, nothing,' they said. He said to them, 'But now if you have a purse, take it, and the same with a haversack; if you have no sword, sell your cloak and buy one.'[7]

Whatever view you take of violence, this passage is rather odd. It appears only in Luke and seems to have little connection with what Luke places before and after it. At most, it could be used to argue that Jesus considered it acceptable to carry a sword when travelling, perhaps out of fear of attack. This is very different from the acceptance of warfare and armies.

The line serves as a reminder to avoid simplistic generalisations about Jesus' views. However, his words at his arrest seem to be far more consistent with his other teachings than the line encouraging the disciples to carry swords (see Chapter 15 for other examples of Jesus' comments on using violence). This being so, it is the pro-sword comment, rather than the anti-sword comment, that seems out of place.

Following his arrest, Jesus was handed over to the Roman authorities. He was condemned to death by crucifixion by Pontius Pilate, the Roman governor of Judea. Crucifixion, one of the most painful deaths that human cruelty has ever invented, was used by the Romans largely on political troublemakers.

Given that Jesus knew that this awaited him, his decision not to resort to violence is all the more striking. It's difficult to get away from Jesus' last words to his followers before his death: 'Put your sword back.'

QUESTIONS

1. Was Jesus rejecting the use of weapons in all circumstances or only some?
2. What do Jesus' words and behaviour at his arrest say about his beliefs and the way he understood his mission?
3. Jesus was executed by the Roman Empire as a political troublemaker. How does this affect our choices if we seek to follow Jesus today?

NOTES

1   Mark 13:34–37.
2   Luke 22:44.
3   W.D. Davies and Dale C. Allison, *Matthew: A Shorter Commentary* (T & T Clark International, 2004).
4   Morna Hooker, *The Gospel According to St Mark* (A & C Black, 1991).
5   Ched Myers, *Binding the Strong Man: A Political Reading of Mark's Story of Jesus* (Orbis Books, 1988).
6   Stanley Hauerwas, *Matthew* (SCM Press, 2006).
7   Luke 22:35–36.

18. Where next?

I sometimes imagine Jesus being interviewed on a political discussion programme on the BBC. He might not make a great interviewee. His refusal to give direct answers must have infuriated some of his listeners. It continues to frustrate people now.

There are many things that can be said about Jesus' obtuse way of responding to questions. It was a common rhetorical practice among Jews at the time. He was trying to dodge verbal traps. Perhaps he was avoiding the danger of arrest. It also seems likely that Jesus wanted people to think.

I am sometimes told the Bible is 'clear' and that all we have to do is to 'do what it says'. If Jesus had taken this approach, would he not have given direct answers and clear commands?

In writing this book, I had to resist the temptation to try to summarise Jesus' ideas in neat points and to present you with my overall analysis of his thoughts. Jesus' original listeners did not encounter him in this way. They may have heard a snatch of debate, an interesting question, a thought-provoking parable. Some would have gone on their way and thought little of it. Others may have decided to find out more.

Occasionally, when I have given a talk about Jesus, I have been asked to recommend books about him. I am always delighted that someone is interested enough to want to explore Jesus further. And I can certainly recommend long lists of books. But if you are reading about Jesus for the first time, there is a more useful book to begin with.

Read the Bible.

It sounds obvious, but many people who want to read *about* Jesus' teachings are rather nervous of just getting on and reading Jesus' teachings themselves. Of course, they may want guidance. They may want to know about context, history, language. That's fair enough; these things will help. But start with Jesus' words, or the words written about him shortly after his lifetime.

If you have rarely or never opened the New Testament, then I suggest starting with Mark's Gospel, which is the shortest and has the fastest pace as a story. You will see how some of Jesus' teachings fit together with each other, with his actions and with what's going on around him. The other gospels are also worth reading of course, along with the rest of the writings in the New Testament, which wrestle with the meaning of Jesus. I also love the Hebrew scriptures (known as the Old Testament), though I admit to knowing far less about them.

When reading, don't worry if there are parts you really struggle with – keep going and then turn back later to look at the troubling bits. Take time to think about your own reactions. Don't feel bad if you feel confused, worried or angry. Then perhaps it's time to ask others what they think or to read more about what you find there.

In the list of suggested reading at the back of this book, you will find some information on different translations of the Bible, as well as suggested books and websites about particular themes related to Jesus and his ideas.

There are many different takes on the meaning of Jesus' teaching. To me, it seems that Jesus is always encouraging us to make choices. Shall we serve God or Mammon? What belongs to God and what belongs to Caesar? Is God's will found in the nobleman or the rebellious servant? Should we follow the law-breaker or the legalist, the Samaritan or the lawyer? Do we trust in the power of the sword or the power of love and justice?

Whether you are new to thinking about Jesus or have been doing so for years, I hope this book has given you something to think about.

The book would not have been possible without dozens of

people who shared their thoughts on the passages in question. It seems appropriate that they should have the last word. I asked some of them how they felt about Jesus as a result of their reading. Here are the answers.

'Some of the passages made Jesus really stand out as a rebel against the establishment. Some of them are so alien to how I live that it makes no sense to me.' – Jennifer

'Well, I wouldn't say it's altered my perceptions of Jesus. Biblical stories can't be taken as face-value accounts of Jesus – many, perhaps most, are apocryphal. That said, if those stories are broadly reflective of the views Jesus and his supporters espoused, it would explain how Christianity became popular among the poor of the time. Perception is more important than reality.' –Chaminda

'I don't think it's changed my perception of Jesus as such but has reminded me of how deep some of the teachings are, and how much they ask of us. It's not easy, to be Love and to serve from that sacred place. It also reminded me of the resonance between the teachings of Jesus, and those of essential Islam/ Sufism.' – Fatimah

'Being full of love doesn't seem to make Jesus happy. I suppose that's my abiding image of him from this experience – righteously angry, idealistic, misunderstood, speaking in language too abstract to be understood by those around him, and disappointed; the things people do make him sad.' – Samantha

'Jesus' words are critical of the very ideals that we find in modern capitalism. To me, these teachings support more strongly the ideals of socialism, that we pay people fairly, that we don't exploit the workers who provide the means for production and the creation of wealth, and that we contribute what we can and take only what we need.' – Carl

'Largely pro-religion, I found it surprising how much of the passages I took offence to. Christianity does a lot of good for many people and I've a huge amount of respect for religion on the whole so I don't wish to belittle Christianity at all. But from what I can see the Bible reads terribly from a modern feminist perspective! If Jesus is the ultimate role model, then surely we should question him the most?' – Louise

'I think I have a much stronger sense of Jesus as a human I can relate to. I think that's perhaps because of how often he is put on the spot and having to be quick-witted to get himself out of attempted traps gracefully! This seems very human. His teachings seem incredibly powerful and challenging, but it feels like the most challenging passages, particularly on how to relate to otherness and difference, are not at the forefront of our collective consciousness as a self-professedly Christian society. I wonder how leading politicians would have been affected by being interviewed on these passages?' – Beccy

'I realised how little I knew about what Jesus is reported to have said and done, beyond being born and dying. I found he was quite a radical, and more subversive than I had thought. And he encouraged people to think for themselves. I always had an airy idea of someone gazing up to the sky being super gentle and softly spoken all the time.' – Elinor

The Upside-down Bible

Suggested reading

BIBLES

If you are new to the Bible and want to read it (or some of it), there is a bewildering variety of English translations from which to choose. The version most often quoted in this book is the *New Jerusalem Bible* (*NJB*), although at times I have quoted from the *New Revised Standard Version* (*NRSV*). The NRSV is the translation generally used by academics and students in the UK.

I also recommend *Good as New*, a translation of the New Testament by John Henson. It is a much looser translation, seeking to translate Jesus' words into our own culture as well as our own language. While this may be a problem if you want to think about the original precise meaning, it gives the New Testament a freshness and liveliness that some versions lack. Henson's translation also takes account of Jesus' radical challenge to wealth and power.

Other reasonable translations include the *New International Version* (*NIV*) and the *New English Bible* (*NEB*). The most famous English translation is the *King James Bible*, also known as the *Authorised Version* (*AV*). This was the version used by most British churches from the early seventeenth century until well into the twentieth. However, the use of seventeenth-century language makes it difficult to read at times, while some of the translation is rather questionable.

Translations to avoid include the *Good News Bible* (*GNB*). The GNB waters down much of the text, choosing translations that ignore the political significance of the original. Similar criticisms can be made of *The Message*, which at times does a good job of turning the text into colloquial US English, but often at the expense of political meaning.

JESUS, HIS TEACHINGS AND THEIR RELEVANCE TODAY

Sarah Bessey, *Jesus Feminist: An Invitation to Revisit the Bible's View of Women* (Darton, Longman & Todd, 2013)

Paul Buhle, Sabrina Jones and others, *Radical Jesus: A Graphic History of Faith* (Herald Press, 2013)

Deirdre Good, *Jesus' Family Values* (Seabury Press, 2006)

Keith Hebden, *Seeking Justice: The Radical Compassion of Jesus* (Circle Books, 2013)

Amy-Jill Levine, *Short Stories by Jesus: The Enigmatic Parables of a Controversial Rabbi* (HarperCollins, 2014)

Noel Moules, *Fingerprints of Fire, Footprints of Peace: A Spiritual Manifesto from a Jesus Perspective* (Circle Books, 2012)

Walter Wink, *Jesus and Nonviolence: A Third Way* (Augsburg Fortress, 2003)

WHAT CAN WE KNOW ABOUT JESUS?

David Boulton, *Who on Earth was Jesus? The Modern Quest for the Jesus of History* (O Books, 2008)

Anthony Le Donne, *Historical Jesus: What Can We Know and How Can We Know It?* (William B Eerdmans, 2011)

BOOKS ON READING THE BIBLE

Simon Jenkins, *The Bible from Scratch: A Lightning Tour from Genesis to Revelation* (Lion Books, 2009)

Lloyd Pietersen, *Reading the Bible after Christendom* (Paternoster, 2011)

Ray Vincent, *Let the Bible be Itself: Learning to Read it Right* (O Books, 2008)

RELEVANT INFLUENTIAL TEXTS

William Countryman, *Dirt, Greed and Sex: Sexual Ethics in the New Testament and their Implications for Today* (SCM Press, 2011)

Elisabeth Schussler Fiorenza, *In Memory of Her: A Feminist Theological Reconstruction of Christian Origins* (Crossroad Publishing, 1994)

Norman K. Gottwald and Richard A. Horsley (eds.), *The Bible and Liberation: Political and Social Hermeneutics* (Orbis Books/ SPCK, 1993)

Ched Myers, *Binding the Strong Man: A Political Reading of Mark's Story of Jesus* (Orbis Books, 1988)

R. S. Sugirtharajah (ed.), *The Postcolonial Biblical Reader* (Blackwell Publishing, 2006)

WEBSITES

There are uncountable hundreds of websites devoted to discussion of the Bible, Christianity and related topics. Many of the most interesting are individual blogs and small-scale sites, so it is well worth exploring the web to find sites and discussions that particularly interest you.

The following may be helpful.

Bible Gateway (https://www.biblegateway.com) includes the texts of most English translations (but not the *New Jerusalem Bible*), and many in other languages. This allows you to compare the wording chosen by different translations.

New Testament Gateway (http://www.ntgateway.com) includes the texts of several different translations along with helpful links to articles and essays about aspects of the New Testament.

Ekklesia (http://www.ekklesia.co.uk) is a Christian think-tank with an online news service. It seeks to explore Christianity in a post-Christendom society. Articles and news on the site include discussions of Jesus and his relevance today.

Ship of Fools (http://www.ship-of-fools.com) is a Christian community and discussion site. It includes satire and humour as well as serious articles and lively discussions. Debates over the meaning of Jesus' teachings often feature.

The Upside-down Bible